PICTORIAL HISTORY
OF CARS

PICTORIAL HISTORY OF CARS

PETER ROBERTS

Sundial

Contents

Acknowledgments

The author wishes to express his gratitude for help in
supplying documents, photographs and information to:
Adam Opel AG; Alfa Romeo SpA; Mr. John Conde of the
American Motors Corporation; Antique Automobile Club of
America Inc.; Aston Martin (1975) Limited; Audi NSU
Auto Union AG; Automobiles Peugeot; Mr. Cecil Bendall;
British Leyland Limited; Burberrys Limited; Chrysler
United Kingdom and USA; The Craven Foundation, Canada;
Daimler-Benz AG; Detroit Public Library, Historic
Collection; Dunlop Limited; Fiat SpA; Ford Motor Co Limited
and Mrs. S. Knapman; Ford Motor Co of America; Henry Ford
Museum; General Motors in UK and USA; Mercedes-Benz
(UK) Limited; Michelin Tyre Co Limited; Motor Vehicle
Manufacturers Association USA; Régie Nationale des
Usine Renault; Rolls-Royce Motors Limited; R.A.C.; Science
Museum; Shell UK Oil and Mr. Philip Jaques; Société
Citroën; The Transport Trust; Vauxhall Motors Limited;
Volkswagen (GB) Limited; Woolf, Laing, Christie &
Partners; Mr. Michael Worthington-Williams.

First published in Great Britain by
Sundial Publications Limited, 59 Grosvenor Street London W1
Revised 1978

© 1977 Hennerwood Publications Limited
ISBN 0 904230 26 0

Produced by Mandarin Publishers Limited
22a Westlands Road, Quarry Bay, Hong Kong
Printed in Hong Kong

Foreword

My qualification for writing the
foreword to the Pictorial History of Cars is that
I earn my living by driving motor cars rather
fast. Many people think that the sort of cars I race
bear no resemblance whatsoever to anything that
is discussed in these pages; the basic concept
does, however, remain the same and the component
and tyre manufacturers still use racing and
rallying to improve standards for the ordinary
road cars.
I therefore owe a lot to the motor car.
I have never had time to study its history in great
detail and it is only when looking through the
pages of Peter Roberts' book that I realise fully the
vast strides that have been made in its
development in a relatively short period.
I am going to enjoy learning more about
the motor car and I feel honoured to have been asked
to be associated with this excellent book.

James Hunt

THE INVENTORS

When the automobile made its appearance towards the end of the last century, it was the natural outcome of practical experiments made by many men. The car was an amalgamation of some of the best of them – a hybrid of ideas taken from railway locomotive engineering, horse carriage design, and the more recent bicycle industry. No single person was responsible, although Benz and Daimler, both Germans, did produce the first practicable petrol-driven cars; and the first successes were the result of slow progress towards an old goal – the making of a vehicle propelled by its own machinery – and they were achieved earlier than most of us imagine . . .

The scene, a tree-lined Paris square; the date, 1769, just over 200 years ago. Cobblestones echoed to the clatter of carriages and the clop of hooves. The gentry strutted the streets in brocade and lace, while peasants from the surrounding countryside sold their produce to passers-by. Louis XVI was on the throne of France. In Corsica, the infant Napoleon Bonaparte lay in his cradle; the French Revolution was still twenty years away.

Suddenly, the usual street noise was drowned by a heavier sound. People paused to listen. From a narrow street, a huge wood-and-metal monster clanked and lurched into the square, its great iron-shod wooden wheels, taller than a grown man, grinding over the cobbles. A jet of steam hissed from a witch's cauldron at the front of the machine. On a small seat high in the vehicle sat a man heaving on an iron lever, striving desperately to keep his machine on the road. The age of motoring had almost dawned.

Since the days of ancient Greece, mechanical power had been the dream of engineer, politician, soldier and traveller. The Greeks themselves invented a primitive turbine, a metal sphere containing water which when heated escaped as steam through small pipes, forcing the sphere to rotate.

Through the centuries, there were to be many attempts to build a self-propelled road transport machine. Some were designed to use the elements – wind, water, fire. From clockwork springs to falling weights, from hopefully conceived perpetual motion to compressed air and vacuum, men of vision or hope applied their various sciences – the Jesuit priests, German clock-makers, the inventors of France and Italy – all with varying degrees of failure. But the names of these men – Huygens, Volta, the great Leonardo, Father Verbiest (who had as good a claim as any to actually building the first steam model), Hans Hautsch, Du Quet, Newcomen – all belong among those whose work was later used by the engineers who finally created the mechanically propelled vehicle.

One of the first experimenters was a young Frenchman, Denis Papin, who in 1698 adopted a gunpowder-propellant principle after a Dutchman had failed in an earlier attempt to move a vehicle in this way. Papin sensibly abandoned this

violent fuel for steam. He built his model engine in the belief that "this innovation may be used with advantage for other ends than raising water, and I made a model of a small chariot which moved itself by means of this force . . . I believe (however) that the inequalities and twisting of the main roads will make it difficult to develop this invention for use in land carriages." He did, however, apply his logic to the field of marine power.

During the 17th century there were numerous, highly non-technical treatises on the theme of the self-propelled vehicle, most of them in a similar vein: ". . . divers engines that do without horse move carriages to plough landes and make voyages upon the oceans as swifte as boates that sayl in faire windes." However it was not until the following century, on that sunny morning in pre-revolution Paris, that the first mechanically propelled vehicle actually performed. Nicholas Joseph Cugnot, who must be recognized as father of a new world of transport, was the builder and driver of the steam dinosaur, which was in fact a full-size prototype of his lightweight model made six years earlier. Although stationary steam engines were now employed for pumping and winching, it was a couple of generations before the first railway was to be seen and twenty years before the first steam-boat was built.

Cugnot's steam gun-carriage worked after a fashion at a full two miles an hour, with enforced stops every 15 minutes to re-build pressure. He made a second with a larger boiler. It was never officially recognized, but the steam dray (*fardier à vapeur*) was nonetheless tested, hauled a sizeable load – and finally caused the world's first motor accident by demolishing a wall.

Cugnot's name remains first in the list of road transport builders, but little came of his work in France. Louis XVI and Marie Antoinette went in a horse-drawn tumbril to the guillotine and Napoleon gave little thought to steam-drawn gun carriages during his career.

THE BRITISH CONNECTION

About twenty years later, the steaming, clanking pre-dawn of motoring moved to England. William Murdock, a pupil of the engineer James Watt (who improved the steam engine) had seen Cugnot's plans. He learnt from the Frenchman's prime mistake by designing a model steam three-wheel loco with the engine over the rear wheels to improve stability. This small model first ran in 1784 near Murdock's home in Redruth, Cornwall. On one occasion when he was testing it at dusk, the machine ran hissing and sparking past the vicar who, predictably enough, thought the Devil was paying a short

PREVIOUS PAGES: The first Benz advertisement was in brochure form, giving few details of the mechanism of the vehicles. This engraving from a prospectus, published in 1888, described the car as a "pleasant carriage that would run on naphtha, paraffin or petrol which would climb hills of more than a gradient of 1 in 16 when loaded or 1 in 12 when unladen".

visit to the town. Watt, possibly motivated by jealousy, took Murdock off the project. Certainly Murdock never had time or money enough to build a full-sized version.

It was another Cornishman, Richard Trevithick, who became father of road transport in Britain. A mining engineer, Trevithick had presumably seen Murdock's little steam-devil – he lived only four miles from Redruth – and decided to construct a high-pressure engine moved by steam. On Christmas Eve, 1801, he rolled it out for its first test – it was little more than a boiler on wheels – and took a number of friends aboard for the ride. "When we see'd that Captain Dick was agoing to turn on steam, we jumped up, as many as could, maybe seven or eight of us. 'Twas a stiffish hill, but she went off like a bird . . ." On its first outing the contraption steamed half a mile up a hill "at a pace faster than a man could walk . . ."

Trevithick and his friends were not destined to enjoy many jaunts in the prototype. On one early run, they stopped at a hostelry for a convivial glass, forgetting to douse the boiler fire. England's first motor carriage was destroyed by the flames.

The dogged Cornishman built another carriage – one that looked like a real carriage this time, and drove it through

ABOVE: England in the first half of the 19th century saw a number of steam coaches chuffing about urban roads at speeds up to 25 km/h (15 mph) and carrying paying passengers. This one was designed by Gurney to run on the London–Bath route. It made one trip.

LEFT: A steam carriage in trouble on the road, 1836. Some of the steam coaches of the 1830's were reliable enough to make reasonably long journeys over country routes, most of which were maintained under England's "turnpike" system.

London's Oxford Street on demonstration runs. Nobody was interested, so he sold the power unit to a miller. He then switched his attention to railway locomotives and stationary engines, units which were very much smaller than earlier examples. Samuel Homfrey, proprietor of an ironworks in South Wales, employed one of the latter to operate a steam hammer, later attaching wheels so that it could travel up and down the rails of a crude tramway.

RAIL OR STEAM BUS?

Although railways were born a few years later, and had become the standard method of travel by the 1840's, road communication in Britain might have developed much more rapidly if steam power had been permitted to flourish on the highways.

Post-Napoleonic-war trade had increased and Britain's goods and passenger transport needs bred better roads. The work of Macadam and Telford brought such improvements that long-distance coaching travel had become routine for merchants and government officials. They

LEFT: Cugnot's steam-driven wagon of 1769 was a three-wheeled monster carrying a front-mounted boiler and a two cylinder engine – all located over the front wheel. Its shambling 2 miles an hour top speed did not prevent it causing the first motor accident when it ran out of control and demolished a garden wall.

also enabled coaching companies to set up country-wide networks of regular services.

At this time, in the 1820's, several engineers had turned their thoughts to a self-propelled coach. Steam coach companies were formed, and soon operated in competition with the horse-drawn coaching groups and the railways. However, they were soon hounded off the roads of Britain by those whose interests were in rail and horse-drawn transport; swingeing tolls were also a factor – most of the country was under the turnpike – and the steam coaches came to a grinding halt. What could have bloomed into a flourishing road transport industry was virtually smothered at birth. In 1865, the Light Locomotive of Highways Act, which required a man carrying a red flag to walk in front of a mechanically propelled vehicle, finished the steam coach companies for ever.

It is worth contemplating what would have been the situation of Britain's motor industry at the end of the last century if steam transport had been allowed to develop unhampered by the coaching interests and railway investors. In the event, the horse-coaching companies also perished, for the new railway network became so popular and cheap that by mid-Victorian times the great coaching days were but memories to the ageing. For a while, nothing replaced the coach, and grass began to grow over the roads

of the country, farmers quietly extended their fields over the highways, and the once-flourishing arteries narrowed down to the single tracks of medieval days.

In any case, steam would have eventually given way to another more manageable power, gasoline. Oil mining and refining had produced a by-product in petroleum spirit, and its near-explosive qualities were soon to be harnessed by inventive engineers. Also, metals were becoming more durable and reliable and, probably most significant of all developments, engineers had developed lathes that could bore a near-perfect round hole in a block of steel.

Stationary engines using town gas had been in use regularly since 1860. Enormous, inefficient, and usable only where there was a piped supply of gas, the first engines of this type were designed for use without a compression stroke. Veritable mountains of metal, producing mice-power, they were nevertheless the first practical internal combustion engines.

A Frenchman, Jean Etienne Lenoir, built the first practical gas engine and later produced a smaller version, using it to power a form of car by means of a vaporized liquid fuel. In 1862 he ran it the half-a-dozen miles between his place of work and home. Next, a German, Dr. Nikolaus Otto, who had studied Lenoir's "mobile engine", was inspired to improve on it. He developed the "Otto Cycle" or

four-stroke system, which he patented in an attempt to corner the future market. Like so many others, the patent was overthrown by hard-headed successors in the motor industry.

Otto's engine was a great improvement on Lenoir's, employing the four strokes of a modern engine – a downward induction stroke, the piston drawing in the fuel-air mix; an upward compression stroke to concentrate the mixture in the cylinder head; a power stroke when the fuel is ignited and expands rapidly; followed by an exhaust stroke during which the burnt gases are expelled. It was the compression stroke that made the big difference, producing a great deal more energy from a smaller engine: an engine small enough to be installed in a carriage.

FATHERS OF THE AUTOMOBILE

In Germany two men were moving slowly towards building the first practical automobile. Although their backgrounds were different their careers were curiously similar: both had worked on stationary gas engines and lived in the same region of Germany. Their projects were similar although their methods were different, and they both produced their first motor vehicles within a few months of each other – quite independently and without any knowledge of each other's work.

Karl Benz had started a small business making gas engines in Mannheim, and by 1879 had made his most advanced

prototype petrol engine. Benz wrote of the moment that was to turn a page of history. It was New Year's Eve 1879, "After supper my wife said, 'Let's go over to the shop and try our luck once more. Something tells me to go and will not let me be.' So there we were back again standing over the engine as if it were a great mystery that was impossible to solve. My heart was pounding. I turned the crank. The engine started to go put-put-put, and music of the future sounded with regular rhythm. We both listened to it for a full hour, fascinated, never tiring of the single tone of its song. The longer it played its note, the more sorrow and anxiety it conjured away from the heart."

"Suddenly the bells began to ring – New Year's Eve bells. We felt they were not only ringing in a new year but a new era, which was to take on a new heart-beat . . ." Karl Benz and his young wife Bertha could hardly have made a more accurate forecast.

In 1885 the first three wheeled patent motor car, based largely on bicycle construction principles, and with the little one cylinder engine tucked away behind the seat, wobbled around the courtyard of the Mannheim workshop with Benz "as proud as a king to see finally my youthful dream standing before me."

Three years later Benz was advertising "An agreeable vehicle as well as a mountain-climbing apparatus" to the public. The public declined to buy – until

BELOW: Although steam as a propellant for road vehicles gave way to the more manageable fuel, gasoline, the transition was gradual. Early steam enthusiast Comte Albert de Dion persuaded mechanical toymakers Bouton and his brother-in-law Trepardoux to join him in a full-size steam vehicle project. Their first model, a quadricycle, was working by 1883, and was followed by several heavier vehicles. This is one of some four years later.

BOTTOM LEFT: In Bad Cannstatt, Germany, Gottlieb Daimler fitted his first petrol engine, a $\frac{1}{2}$ horsepower one cylinder unit using "hot tube" ignition, into a boneshaker cycle frame, using it as a test-bed.

BOTTOM CENTRE: Daimler's 1885 vehicle, the first four-wheeled horseless carriage. It trundled its stout owner first round the courtyard of the little works then out into the streets of Cannstatt. Daimler's main interest was in his engine and he used it to propel a small airship, a tram, a fire-engine, and a river boat within months of the first trials.

BOTTOM RIGHT: This 1894 Benz Velo was the first motor car in the world to be produced in quantity for the public, and soon became the best known of all Benz cars up to that date.

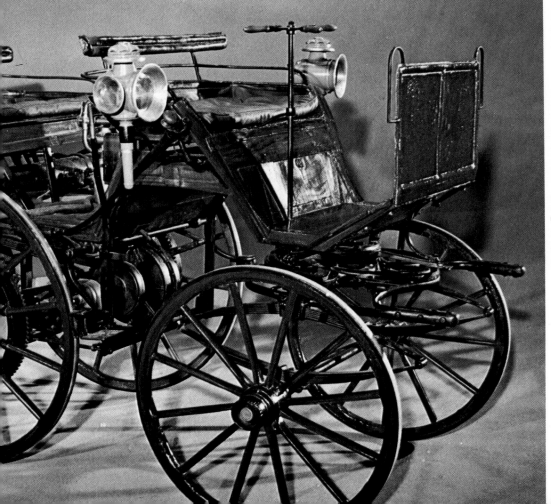

his family took a hand. Early one August morning in 1888, while father Benz was still asleep, his sons Eugen and Richard and their mother "stole" the car from the workshop and set off for Pforzheim, over a hundred kilometres distant. With the boys (aged 15 and 13) at the tiller they drove the frail car through countryside and towns, buying benzin (petroleum spirit) from apothecaries, and once, leather for a worn-out brake from a cobbler. They pushed the car up gradients and coasted down shallow hills. It was dark when they arrived at Pforzheim, where they telegraphed Karl and explained the mysteries of the car to a fascinated crowd. One or two onlookers pessimistically forecast that now they could all sell their draught animals to the local horse-butcher. This, the first long-distance journey by motor, coupled with the Munich exhibition the following year, began to bring in orders for the Benz vehicle.

WÜRTTEMBERG VISIONARY

In 1886, Gottlieb Daimler bought his wife Emma an unusually lavish birthday gift, a four-seater phaeton. It was, in Daimler's own words, "Handsomely and solidly built" and was to be delivered in secret and presented to his wife as a surprise.

The arrangement was in fact a deception, for when the phaeton was safely in Daimler's Cannstatt workshop, he stripped off the shafts, installed a steering linkage and a tiny, single cylinder, one horsepower (hp) internal combustion engine of his own design.

The first four-wheeler automobile was born. Daimler had tried out his engine a few months earlier on a "boneshaker" bicycle, and once he had established the fact that it would actually propel a vehicle he determined to install a slightly larger one in a passenger-carrying carriage. Unlike the Benz tricycle, which was built without reference to coach tradition, this was a true horseless carriage.

Daimler's vehicle employed innovations and principles that were to be bought, copied or built under licence for many years. The engine was rubber-mounted to reduce road shock, it had fan cooling, a friction clutch, a mixture preheated by the exhaust gases, a two-speed gearbox and a sophisticated differential. It clattered along the streets of Cannstatt at up to 18 km/h (11 mph) – the speed of a fast trot.

However, Daimler's main preoccupa-tion was not with road transport, but with an engine that could "power many different aspects of travel or industry." The stocky Württemberger installed his single-cylinder vertical engine in a river boat (still at the Daimler-Benz museum in Stuttgart for visitors to see), telling enquirers that it was electrically propelled, and mystifying the entire town. A local newspaper report ran: "Recently a boat has been circulating on the Necker . . . it appears to be driven by some unseen power up and down stream with great speed, causing astonishment to bystanders."

A couple of years later, Daimler had tried out his engine in an airship (it made a flight of four kilometres) and the high speed unit was rapidly becoming popular for bench-saws, fire pumps and even street cars. As a concession to road travel, he went on to design with his partner Wilhelm Maybach a light car they called the "Steel Wheeler" which departed – in the direction of bicycle design – from traditional carriage construction. This was built around the new Daimler two-cylinder V engine which produced twice the power of the first unit.

The 1889 Paris World Fair boosted the Daimler fortunes. His engine caught the imagination of Messieurs Panhard and Levassor who drew up contracts to build it under licence in France. With both Benz and Daimler selling their products it seemed that Germany was to be the leading nation in the new automobile world. However, with the building of the first Panhard-Levassor cars, France became the centre of motoring interest.

It took just a couple of years for Armand Peugeot, son of a large ironmongery-manufacturing family who had also made cycles and steam cars, to show an interest in the automobile. In 1891 he made his first car, using a Panhard engine and testing it by following a long-distance cycle race in northern France.

By now, rivalry between steam-driven and petrol-driven cars was intense – and the score was about even. The electric car, silent and reliable, was also popular, and indeed the first vehicle to set a world speed record, driven in 1898 by Count Chasseloup-Laubat at 62.8 km/h (39 mph) was electrically powered. He was challenged on several runs by another electric car driven by the ebullient Camille Jenatzy. Steam cars had been familiar on French roads for a number of years, produced by the workshops of Bollée, Serpollet, and De Dion, Bouton et Cie.

In 1894 the motor-racing era was flagged

off. The first motor-sport event included entries from the workshops of Benz (the Velo, recognized as the world's first standard production car was selling well) and Daimler (his 4 hp belt-driven cars were in production and his engines used to power Panhards and Peugeots). Among the other entries were sundry steamers, tricycles, and several vehicles whose methods of propulsion were questionable to say the least.

ABOVE: Considered elegant in design and sophisticated in equipment, the Benz "Comfortable", first made in 1898, found a ready market outside its country of origin, Germany. The first Benz to be fitted with pneumatic tyres, the car was built on the same lines as the earlier Velo, but designed for increased driving comfort and running safety.

LEFT: The most decorated car? This early Peugeot vis-à-vis (face-to-face seating) with elaborate ornamentation, was a product of the Peugeot factory at Valentigney. The model housed a $3\frac{3}{4}$ hp V-twin engine of 1018 cc under the seat of the *conducteur*, which would propel the car at a satisfactory 30 km/h ($18\frac{1}{2}$ mph) in 1892.

ABOVE: A Peugeot phaeton, 1894, in competition trim, with crew. This 2 horse-power four-seater with its V-twin Daimler engine at the rear was a contestant in the Paris-Rouen Trial of 1894.

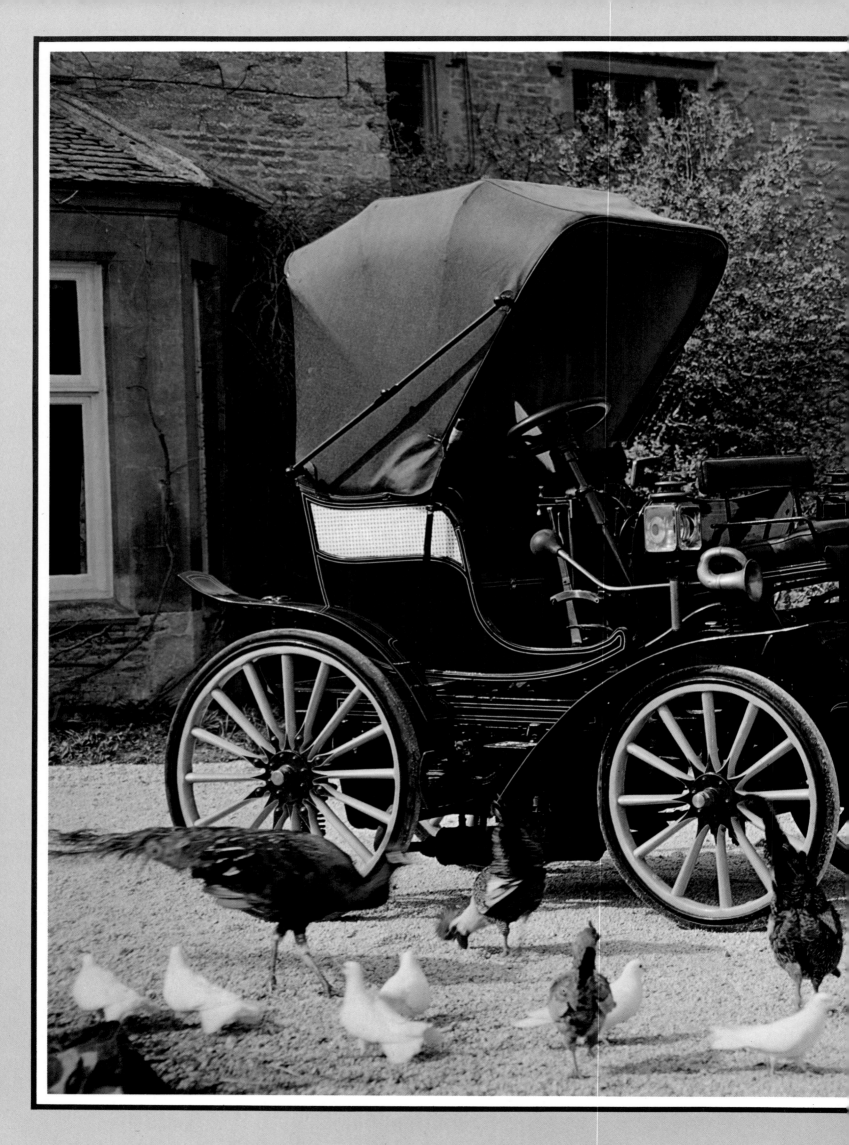

Carriage Trade

Motoring had been received in France with open arms and there was none of the suspicion and reluctance to accept the new machinery that impeded the early growth of the industry elsewhere. A major factor in the spread of the automobile in France was the fine network of long, straight and well-surfaced roads that Napoleon had laid down for his troops. Another was the much-needed mobility the motor car would bring to a large country whose railways were somewhat underdeveloped.

By the end of the 1800s automobilism (which was only one of a number of awkward terms for motoring) had become established in France with a small and fairly wealthy group of enthusiasts, who treated this new mobility, not yet proven as a reliable method of transport, purely as a sport. Said one automobilist to the press: "One hunts in cold, damp weather, and when it is dry and hot, one motors. To each its appropriate time." Others found the motor car most convenient for short, domestic journeys. "One could place the vehicle beside the stream," reads a contemporary French journal "and after piscatorial success travel swiftly to the evening *billiard* at home." Such was the role of the car in 1894.

The first French models were small and light, with tiny, one-cylinder engines. But slowly, the cylinders multiplied, power output rose, and with Panhard's fortuitous front-engine rear-drive layout followed by the development of the de Dion high speed engine in 1895, the essentials of future design were rapidly laid. Later developments were firmly built on these early foundations.

It was inevitable that France should produce the first automobile empire. Its Louis Renault produced in his garden shed a machine based on a de Dion tricycle to which he added a fourth wheel.

Success came almost as a surprise.

well ahead of the time in several respects. It had overcome the clumsiness of the current belt-drive by taking the drive through a three-speed gearbox and shaft to a differential back axle, and had a patented, direct drive in top gear. Built on a tubular chassis, it broke with the traditional carriage design.

Within six months, Louis and his brothers had made and sold 60 voiturettes and introduced the first saloon car to the public. In the next two years they successfully competed in a number of motor races (this was the time of the epic city-to-city events), exhibited their cars all over Europe and employed 110 workers.

Armand Peugeot began making his own twin-cylinder engines in 1896 (he too had been using the Daimler patent engine) and in 1900 introduced the front-engine in small- and medium-sized cars which he made at Valentigney. The first was a five to eight hp *tonneau* similar in appearance to the de Dion of the period. The cars of Georges Richard, another motor manufacturer setting up at this time, developed along Benz lines rather than Daimler, and the Paris boulevards echoed to the *teufteuf* of Darraqs, Decauvilles, Delahayes, de Dions, De Dietrichs and by 1904 to the purr of the regal Delaunay – Bellevilles among others.

Louis arrived on his new voiturette at a Christmas Eve party in Paris in 1898. Maître Viot, a friend of the family, begged a ride, and was taken for a spin up the hill to the Butte Montmartre. Pulling 40 louis from his pocket he slapped them on a table and became Renault's first client. Before the evening was over, every man present had been given a demonstration trip – and had put down his deposit. Louis Renault – who was 22 – went home with orders for 12 new cars.

With his brothers Marcel and Fernand, Louis formed a company, moved out of the garden shed and began production; the total equipment was a few lathes, a screw cutting machine, a grinder and a gear cutter.

The design of the spindly little voiturette – it weighed just 350 kilograms – was

By 1903 France, thanks mainly to Renault Frères, was the world's largest motor manufacturing country, and Louis' empire was still growing. Régie Renault is still France's main motor manufacturer, now under government control.

Meanwhile, motor manufacture proliferated throughout France. Panhard's engineer Arthur Krebs designed a true Panhard two-cylinder engine – Daimler-type units had been used up to 1901 – and in 1904 he produced a four cylinder engine with a capacity of no less than 15.435 litres. But the most impressive of them all was Panhard's 1906 unit, an 18.279 litre monster which was used at the height of the dinosaur racing period when the principle of more litres more power was considered practicable in the development of the car engine.

ITALY

Italy's motor car industry aroused little interest during these last years of the 19th century; two engineers, Lanza and Barnadi, had each made a creditable car, but only Lanza was producing commercially. A firm called Prinetti e Stucchi were also making motor cycles and spindly, light cars with no great success. They are noteworthy mainly for the fact that one of their apprentices was a lad named Ettore Bugatti. There was, however, a small rash of new ventures in 1898–9. Bianchi started building light cars in Milan. Ceirano of Turin was making a small car called the Welleys at his bicycle works. Then a small group of financiers and engineers led by one Giovanni Agnelli (who had been working on an engine he had developed at home), bought the Ceirano plant. Later that year – 1899 – the first F.I.A.T. was trundled out of the factory. It was a tidy car, if a little conservative, with a 679 cc twin rear-mounted engine, face-to-face seating, and a Victoria hood which gave it the appearance of an outsize perambulator.

Nevertheless, its 4.2 hp at 400 rpm and top speed of 35 km/h (22 mph) were good enough to secure it a place in the market of the day.

Like Louis Renault, Agnelli plunged into the world of motor sport in the hope of winning free publicity. He won several events and all the publicity he could handle. Within five years, the Turin works had produced 13 different models, including a 10½ litre 60 hp tourer, and a 75 hp *corsa* (racer) of 14 litres. The Fiat company was on its way to becoming one of the largest manufacturers in the modern world, with a share in its national market of around 90 per cent.

BRITAIN

In turn-of-the-century Britain the infant motor industry, long stunted by the 1865 Act of Parliament that put a footman with a red flag in front of all motor vehicles, had been given its independence by another Act that allowed cars to travel at speeds of up to 19 km/h (12 mph). But in 1895, when a tiny motor show was organized by the pioneer Sir David Salomons, there were probably not a

PREVIOUS PAGES: Promoter Harry Lawson's Great Horseless Carriage Company planned to make cars, and bought a factory next door to the new Daimler works in Coventry. By 1898 the company called itself the Motor Manufacturing Company and was turning out vehicles with a decidedly Daimler flavour. Next year the cars were re-designed; this 1900 phaeton had a two cylinder rear engine.

ABOVE: Like Lanchester, Herbert Austin built his first cars (for the Wolseley Sheep Shearing Company) with little reference to current motor design. Built in 1899 this Wolseley is a 3½ hp car, the first production model from the Birmingham works. It had a one cylinder power unit and semi-circular finned tube radiator. This one competed successfully in Britain's Thousand Miles Trial in 1900.

LEFT: Hohenzollern heyday. Crown Prince Wilhelm, son of Germany's Kaiser, persuades a brace of society ladies to take a spin in his Mercedes tourer, *circa* 1903.

FAR LEFT: The French Peugeot motor company appealed to fashionable Paris with this elegant phaeton made between 1897 and 1902. Its two cylinder horizontal engine and four forward speeds made it one of the more sophisticated models of the turn of the century. In the background are a Daimler-engined omnibus and a wagonette.

17

dozen motor cars in Britain. "Today, November 14 1896, is a red letter day," announced Britain's first motor magazine, *The Autocar*, on the day of the Act. "Not only in the history of automobilism, but in that of England itself, for it marks the throwing open of the highways and byways of our beautiful country to those who elect to travel thereupon in carriages propelled by motors." It was hard for those late Victorians to foresee that their great-grandchildren would have to cope with upwards of 14 million such carriages on the highways of their beautiful country.

Business was stirring in the Midlands. Edward Butler had made his motorcycle, Knight his petrol-engined cart, Harry Lawson, the entrepreneur, had been quietly trying to gather the financial reins of motor manufacturing and marketing into his own hands; after the new Act, his activities were more open. He bought the Daimler rights and set up the Daimler Motor Company in an old cotton mill in Coventry. He bought the patent rights of just about every British company, purchased others from French and German manufacturers, then tried to weld the burgeoning industry into one great combine, the British Motor Syndicate, directed by himself. That he did not succeed was due to lack of engineering experience, the use of untried designs, the

refusal of other British designers to succumb to his patent claims, and his being fooled by one or two clever charlatans.

Daimlers, at first imported, then built under licence, began to appear in Coventry in 1896. A London electric brougham by Bersey could be seen silently driving through the streets. Frederic Lanchester, maker of the first successful four-wheel British car, built his prototype in 1895 and was in production at Birmingham by 1900 with a car designed from the ground up as a motor vehicle, quite uninfluenced by carriage traditions. Herbert Austin, later to make vehicles under his own name, made his first three-wheeler in 1895 and, working for the Wolseley Sheep Shearing Company, rolled out the first production Wolseley in 1899. The Benz-based Star was seen at Wolverhampton, a dogcart by the name of Arrol-Johnston in Glasgow, and a little Swift voiturette from the former sewing machine company in Coventry. The Wolverhampton japanning firm of John Marston bravely started production in 1901 of a curious, diamond-shaped motor vehicle bearing the name of Sunbeam-Mabley.

Thus, by 1901, Britain had tentatively entered the world of automobilism, although its offerings were few and small. At the same time, French Panhards,

Renaults and Mors were competing in the Paris to Berlin race at speeds of up to 105 km/h (65 mph). And this year, 1901, was also the year of the Mercedes.

GERMANY

Emil Jellinek, a diplomat and the Daimler agent for the South of France, had used the name of his 11 year-old daughter Mercedes as a pseudonym for several seasons of motor sport at Nice. "Monsieur Mercedes" had made a respected name for himself at the wheel of 23 hp Daimler Phoenix cars in the La Turbie hill-climbs staged behind Monte Carlo, and the various coastal road races.

The Phoenix was a top-heavy vehicle, and its designer, Wilhelm Maybach, then in charge of Daimler development at Cannstatt, was persuaded to produce a car with a lower centre of gravity and longer wheelbase. It was to be entered in the Nice Week Races in March, 1901. The car that was seen that Spring in Nice was to have a greater influence on the design of future vehicles than any other in the history of automobiles, up to and including the Issigonis Mini of 60 years later.

The new Mercedes won almost everything. Deep was the chagrin in the stables of rivals like Panhard, Napier, Mors, Serpollet and the like. As a contemporary journal said: "The victory of the German

LEFT: British pioneer motorists. This photograph, taken outside Warrington Town Hall on June 4th 1901, shows the start of the 3rd Liverpool Heavy Motor Trials. In 1900, many of the people of Britain were introduced to the motor car when the competitors in the Automobile Club (later the RAC) Thousand Miles Trial toured much of the United Kingdom.

BELOW: This "torpedo" of 1896 was one of the few of American Joel Pennington's promised vehicles that became concrete reality. It was a stark three-wheeler said (by Pennington) to carry nine. He did not specify where.

BELOW LEFT: An 1898 Stephens speeds down the Brighton Road on the annual London–Brighton Commemoration Run.

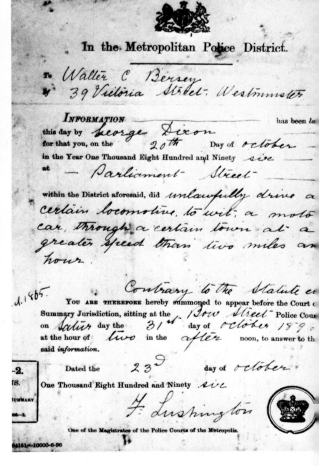

car in the race for speed vehicles is likely to wake up French manufacturers who are disposed to rely too much on their past reputation, and as English, German, Belgian and Austrian makers have now entered the lists, the French firms will have to recognize that there are other firms who can build autocars as well as themselves." During the next few years they all built with a will for an expanding market, copying each other (most of them began to look curiously like the Mercedes) and fitted larger and larger engines in an effort to keep the lead.

The clean sweep specifications of the new Mercedes car were more than merely impressive – they were shattering to an industry still in its experimental stage. Honeycomb radiators had been seen in marine units but here was the coolant tank plus honeycomb design, fitted not as a clumsy waterworks draped in front of the car but as part of the squared-up design of the bonnet. The frame was pressed steel instead of wood, and the flitchplate had vanished. The Mercedes engine was a medium-size 5.9 litre, delivering 35 hp at 1,000 rpm – and had positively operated inlet valves instead of the old type that were opened by the partial vacuum created by the down-sweep of the piston.

There has always been some doubt about the precise date when motorists were first allowed to drive without being preceded by a pedestrian carrying a red flag. However, at least one unfortunate driver fell foul of the Act as late as October 1896.

Pneu Vélo

Michelin

EN VENTE ICI

Affiche à n apposer qu'à l'intérieur du magasin ou garage.

Its four cylinder unit was T-shaped to allow better gas flow, and the gear change was through a gate, not the imprecise quadrant then in use. And of course, the chassis was, for the day, long and low. This car represented the distillation of Maybach's engineering genius and rendered all other marques obsolete during that one glorious week of sport in 1901.

"And," said M. Mercedes, who had promised Maybach to buy the entire first run of this model for sale to the gilded free-spending set in France (as long as he could call it a Mercedes and not the Teutonic-sounding Daimler), "this is as nothing to the automobile you will see next year." He was as good as his word. In 1902, the 40 hp Mercedes Simplex was followed by the legendary 60, the car for which the young bucks of Europe and America would almost sell their grandmothers. "Nous sommes entrés dans l'ère Mercedes," proclaimed a far-sighted French newspaper editorial.

LEFT: An early appearance of the Michelin Man on an advertisement for bicycle tyres.

LEFT: One of the earliest motor cars to be officially called Mercedes (the Daimler-Benz Company of Germany first officially used the name in 1902) this 25/28 hp sports two-seater is dated 1902, although it wears a body made some seven years later.

BELOW: Lady driver, American style – although the steering wheel is still on the right. Left-hand steering wheels first appeared on American cars around 1908. Women at the wheel were rare sights before Charles Kettering developed the electric self-starter for Cadillac in 1911–1912.

BOTTOM: In Germany the sons of sewing machine maker Adam Opel had begun to take an interest in automobiles in 1898, and had produced a Daimler-like vehicle which they sold for 2,900 marks. This one-cylinder tonneau of 1902 was based on a French Darracq chassis on which was mounted an Opel-made body. Top speed was a claimed 45 km/h (28 mph).

CARS IN THE USA

The Birth of Mass Production

T he early development of the automobile in the United States was, in broad historic terms, similar to that which took place in Europe. Steam came first, later to be challenged by electricity and the internal combustion engine, with all three claiming a following for at least ten years into the 20th century. But there were two major differences. The American-built car was never a rich man's toy; and it was built for American conditions. The men who made them were for the most part small-town engineers who worked on their vehicles in the garden shed or in the kitchen on winter evenings. They built their high-wheeled gas buggies for down-to-earth purposes – for farmers, drummers (commercial travellers, whose former transport was the horse and buggy), for doctors, who had suffered like the drummers, and for the grocery store.

As in Europe, mechanical transport had made a genuine start back in the mid-19th century when Richard Dudgeon built a steamer with a coal-fired boiler situated among the passenger seats. Then in 1869 a Roxbury man, Sylvester Roper, amazed his fellow New Englanders by puffing around in his new invention, a steam velocipede.

Towards the end of the 1880s, there were elegant little steam phaetons, with boilers that looked like tea urns, hissing up and down Philadelphia streets. They were functional and almost efficient. But America was not really ready for mechanical propulsion. The masses were farm or industrial workers, who could not afford such luxury.

As soon as Benz or Panhard or Daimler offered their products to the public, a few rich and influential Americans naturally bought one of the new toys to use back at home. But the real American automobile did not develop initially from the German or French product because a different – and more humble – set of people were working on the project of powering a vehicle.

Although the fathers of the American gasoline-fuelled cars are recognized as the Duryea brothers – Frank Duryea drove a gas buggy around Springfield in 1893 – the first primitive engine powered by gasoline was made in 1872. It was built to the heavy proportions of a steam engine, used first in a street car and later as a stationary engine. A young lawyer and Civil War veteran, George Baldwin Selden, saw one, was fascinated and began improving it.

Selden filed a patent for the road vehicle he designed (most records indicate that he never built one) in May 1879, which claimed rights over almost every component used in a motor car. Like Harry Lawson, the English entrepreneur, Selden seemed to have foreseen the birth of the motor industry and planned to benefit from his own contribution. The legal wrangles with manufacturers who declined to pay his royalties lasted a generation until in 1911 Ford finally upset the then notorious Selden Patents. G. B. Selden was a thorn in the side of the early U.S. motor industry, but he did contribute to the basic design of the automobile and has his place in history.

American cars had a functional look from the start. This was not a country of wealthy playboys, but a growing nation whose requirements were mobility to transport goods and to improve commercial communications. The first gener-

ation of vehicles reflected this need, and the other key factor, the continent's appalling roads. Anywhere farther than the next town was a train journey; rail was the only link across the roadless waste.

A few coaching routes provided tenuous links between states, but in winter they became rivers of slime, and in summer choking, dusty, rocky trails, impossible for motor travel. Otherwise, America's roads were either former cattle trails or tracks worn by local use. To be of any use under these conditions, the backyard builders' vehicles were light, with leaf suspension (like on a cart), and high-wheeled, like buggies. The end of the century builders, Duryea, Winton, Olds, Haynes, Apperson and Ford, all reflected the continent's environment in simple but rugged construction. Up to 1900 steam and electric cars also showed this influence; in fact until then no American automobile builder attempted large vehicles on the European scale.

There was not much difference in the popularity of steam, electric and gasoline cars; in 1900 steam was apparently just the more popular in New York, with 1,681 vehicles as against 1,575 electric cars and 936 gasoline machines. Petrol-driven cars were, of course, to be the true inheritors. Steam vehicles, such as those built by the Stanley Brothers, were silent, efficient and simple to drive – but it took minutes to raise steam, they had to be filled with water every few hours and the flues required regular cleaning. Electric cars were also silent but they had to be charged up every 50 miles.

A number of pioneers left steam for internal combustion. Men like Ransom Olds, who had made a steamer in 1887, produced a single-cylinder gasoline engined car in 1896 and formed the Olds Motor Vehicle Company the following year. A fortuitous fire at the factory – the "blessed disaster" his partner called it for reasons of his own – served him well by leaving only one example of a new car left in the gutted works – the Olds Curved Dash. The factory thereafter operated on a one-model policy. In the first year no less than 425 "Merry Olds" bounced off the assembly line, their one cylinder engines giving "one puff to every telegraph pole". By 1902, production was over 2,000 a year, and the Curved Dash became the first mass-produced vehicle, several years before Henry Ford, who is generally considered the originator of mass-production, laid out his moving assembly line at Highland Park.

PREVIOUS PAGES: A Surrey with a fringe on top. This Model C Ford was built about 1905. Developed from the Model A, the C used similar planetary transmission to its illustrious successor, the T.

ABOVE: Sylvester Roper was one of the earliest American inventors of steam buggies and velocipedes, and was shamelessly exploited by a showman named "Professor" W. W. Austen. This advertisement appeared about 1870.

ABOVE: The Curved Dash Oldsmobile, introduced in 1901, was developed from a single prototype which survived a factory fire. It proved utterly reliable and sold in large numbers.

ABOVE: Showing clearly its Locomobile parentage this 1899 Stanley was designed by the famous Stanley twins while they were running a photographic dry plate business in Massachusetts. Having sold the design, they introduced an entirely different model in 1902 with non-condensing engine driving the rear axle direct. This was the forerunner of a long line of famous steamers.

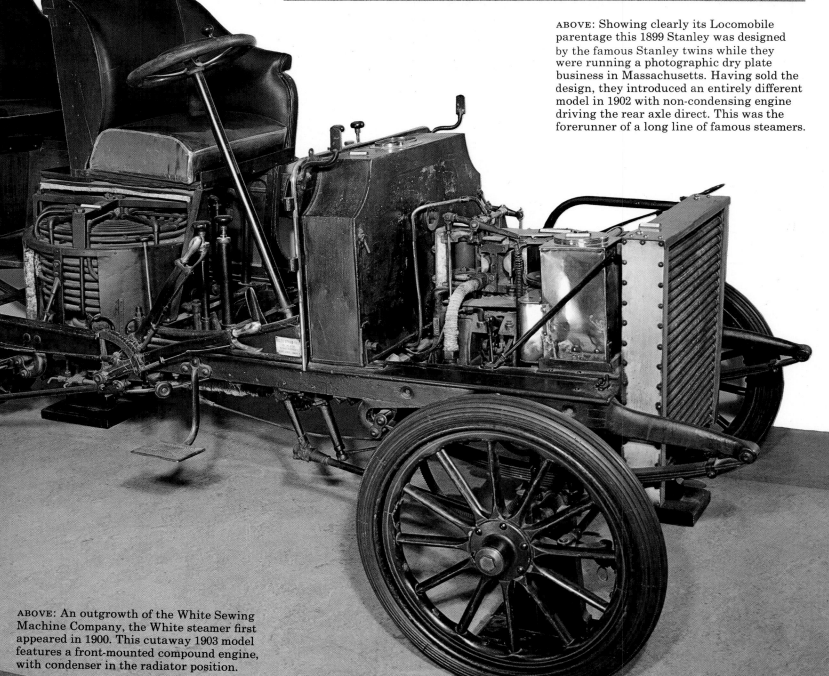

ABOVE: An outgrowth of the White Sewing Machine Company, the White steamer first appeared in 1900. This cutaway 1903 model features a front-mounted compound engine, with condenser in the radiator position.

DETROIT

Detroit in Michigan was soon to become the centre of the new industry, with Ford, Oldsmobile, Buick, Cadillac and Packard) who moved to Detroit from Warren, Ohio, in 1903) as the main manufacturers. In fact 1903 was a memorable year for the motor makers in several ways. Henry Ford opened the Ford Motor Co. that year, having left the Henry Ford Company to be re-organized and re-opened in 1903 by Henry Leland as the Cadillac Automobile Company. The first trans-American trips by car started to convince the public that the automobile was a serious transport proposition; the Peerless Motor Company (formerly a clothes wringer factory) built a car with a pressed steel frame, one of the major advances of the year and one which several others followed shortly afterwards, and Henry Ford was sued for infringing the Selden Patents. This last event caused controversy which eventually freed the American auto industry from some crippling and costly restrictions. By 1906 the American public had settled down to a marked preference for gasoline cars, and design and function were following a recognizable pattern.

Engines in most cars were now at the front, following the Panhard design first seen 16 years earlier in France; the Oldsmobile Curved Dash was an exception, passengers "sitting on the explosion" until 1907. Six cylinder engines were about to become fashionable: Pierce-Arrow, National, Ford, Stevens-Duryea and the air-cooled Franklin now offered them. Maxwell-Briscoe of Terrytown, New York, even made a huge 12 cylinder racing car which, however, failed to make any great mark.

More sophisticated metals were being tried out – high-carbon steel, chrome-

LEFT: New York City, about 1907. The horses have disappeared and parking is already a problem.

ABOVE: Like Jesse Vincent of Packard and Charles Kettering (whose electric self-starter was standard equipment on Cadillacs by 1912), Hugh Chalmers commenced his career in the cash register business. After buying the Thomas-Detroit company he changed the name to Chalmers and this model (*circa* 1910) was one of the first to bear his name. Chalmers also introduced self-starters in 1912.

ABOVE: Peerless, Pierce-Arrow and Packard were once bracketed together as "The three P's" (for prestige) and vied with one another for the bespoke automobile market. This 1909 advertisement, with liveried chauffeur, lives up to the company's slogan "All that the name implies".

nickel, phosphor-bronze, and in 1906 Marmon had used aluminium for the chassis frame in an attempt to save weight. Ford was experimenting with durable vanadium steel, working towards a cheap, simple and rugged car for the multitudes of would-be buyers, mostly small farmers, for whom increased mobility would create prosperity. Henry Ford had been working through the alphabet since his Model A in 1903, and was now at T.

At the time General Motors was founded in 1908, the new industry was in a state of rapid change. Plenty of companies were being established, but for most the pitfalls were too many, and they collapsed as quickly as they came, making little impact. Cars such as the Brush Runabout, the Cole, the Thomas Flyer – well-known names when General Motors was in its infancy – are now remembered by few. Buick, Oldsmobile, Oakland (now Pontiac) and Cadillac formed the nucleus from which the present-day General Motor Corporation has grown.

Ford Touring Car $295

F. O. B. DETROIT
Starter and Demountable Rims $85 Extra

OF all the times of the year when you need a Ford car, that time is NOW!

Wherever you live—in town or country—owning a Ford car helps you to get the most out of life.

Every day without a Ford means lost hours of healthy motoring pleasure.

The Ford gives you unlimited chance to get away into new surroundings every day—a picnic supper or a cool spin in the evening to enjoy the countryside or a visit with friends.

These advantages make for greater enjoyment of life—bring you rest and relaxation at a cost so low that it will surprise you.

By stimulating good health and efficiency, owning a Ford increases your earning power.

Buy your Ford now or start weekly payments on it.

THE MODEL T

Henry Ford said that he had spent the previous 44 years of his life preparing for the Model T, but on 1 October 1908 the American public was unaware that it was about to be fitted with wheels. The Model T Ford – the ugly mule, the Tin Lizzie – was immediately accepted by public and agents alike. "Without doubt," said one enthusiastic dealer, "this is the greatest creation in automobiles ever placed before the people." Production figures for the first year proved him right. More than 10,000 rolled out of the Biquette Avenue Plant at Detroit after a total of about fourteen hours' work on each vehicle. In 1912, the factory was moved to the larger Highland Park plant. When its moving assembly line was complete, the working time on each car had been cut to under an hour, and production for 1912 was nearly ten times that of 1910. By 1914 Ford was producing, with a sixth of America's motor industry labour force, one half of America's cars; Ford was a phenomenon.

It was at this point that Ford – not just an industrialist but a social reformer – was forced to cable his agents instructing them to stop taking orders until further notice. The highly sophisticated plant just could not cope. Ford progressively cut the price of the Model T (following his original principle of bringing the car to the workers) from an initial $850 down (by 1925) to $250, and inaugurated a $5, eight-hour day for all.

Undoubtedly the $5 day, in an age when most auto workers received $2, was economically a dangerous move, but Ford knew it could stop his high labour turnover, that it would create purchasing

ABOVE: Built in a home-workshop behind Henry Ford's home in Bagley Avenue, Detroit, in 1896, the first Ford had a twin cylinder engine, and a combination of chain and belt drive. Early attempts at motor manufacture failed, and Ford's first company (the Detroit Automobile Company) was taken over by H. M. Leland and became Cadillac. The present Ford Motor Company of America was founded in 1903. Ford built the engine himself and first started it while it was bolted to the kitchen sink!

TOP RIGHT: Road conditions near Bloomfield, Connecticut, USA. The car is a Corbin, and the date about 1909.

CENTRE: Although the Model T was built with the conditions prevailing in the early 20th century in mind, the long-lasting qualities were such that it outgrew its era and continued to be made until 1927 when sheer age dictated that it should be supplanted by a more sophisticated model.

LEFT: The kite-shaped brass radiator of this Model T Ford stamps it as having been made before 1917, in which year America entered the war and the T's radiator shell became black-painted steel. Otherwise the basic specification of the car changed little from its introduction in 1908 until the end of its production run. This is a 1910 example.

power for his workers to buy the machines – and that thereby some of the company's high profits would be shared with the employees.

At this time, too, he issued the famous dictum that customers could have "any colour so long as it's black". There was just no time on the assembly lines to provide extra colours. A year or two later Ford thought he would cut prices of the Model T still further, and announced that if his company sold more than 300,000 cars that year he would refund every buyer $50. He finally paid out just over 15 million dollars. The Model T could be seen during these years in a hundred different roles: fitted with flanged wheels to run on railroads; fitted with a hand saw for the timberjack; working as a milking machine; as a pump, and with belts fitted to the jacked-up back wheels to power other machinery. Henry had, it seemed, developed a truly universal tool, one that could last for ever. It almost did – in a 19-year run more than fifteen million Model T automobiles were made by the Ford Motor Company.

Ford's most powerful rival, General Motors, was founded by a former buggy manufacturer, William Crapo Durant. He had tried to purchase the Ford Motor Company but rashly declined to pay the price of $58 million. Durant, undoubtedly a brilliant businessman, was however overwhelmed by the magnitude of the deals, made some errors by buying dud companies and becoming involved in some frauds. Within two years he was in trouble. Henry Leland of Cadillac saved the group by his business and technical expertise, giving a long lease of life to a group whose first principle was to be able to supply any type of car to the public right through the price range, thus competing with the Ford deluge.

THE MODEL T

Henry Ford's amazing company became part of American folklore before it was more than a dozen years old. Songs were written about Fords – often quite independently of the publicity department – verses were composed, jokes appeared about the Model T on matchboxes and in Christmas crackers. Some are admittedly more interesting as history than humour:

"Hear they're magnetizing the Ford's rear axle?"
"Are they; why is that?"
"To pick up all the bits that fall off!"

"Part of a good magician's act is to make a horse vanish. That's nothing though. Look at Henry Ford."

"While other cars passing my cottage
"Are ditched or something goes
    wrong,
"They seldom grow weary of waiting,
"For Fords to tow them along.
"It seems there's always one coming,
"Like the one rattling past them
    before,
"And that's why I never get lonesome
"Where the Fords go by the door."

AMERICAN ROADS

There is another strand to the story of the motor car in the United States, and it is in effect the history of the continent's roads. North America, as several pioneer motorists said, "was easier to sail around than to travel over . . .", and certainly what was called a main road in America would have qualified as a rough country lane in Europe. The roads strongly influenced the design of American cars. Suspension was tough to withstand the battering it received through the wheels; ground clearance was high to avoid wrecking the undergear on boulders and to help get through the vast oceans of mud. Weather protection was virtually nil. It had in fact been neglected in the first flush of enthusiasm, when travellers were fascinated by the element of sport and adventure and simply had not worried.

The first rural concrete road was completed in 1909 on the outskirts of Detroit. Until then there were no more than 480 kilometres (about 300 miles) of American roads with artificial surfaces of any kind – and motoring sportsmen came from far and wide for the pleasure of driving up and down the new road's smooth surface.

Elsewhere in North America, 50 miles in a single day was a gruelling drive, during which the driver might have had to "get out and get under", as the popular song went, two or three times to mend punctures or to lever the car out of some pothole or clamp up a fractured spring. Emergency supplies were standard equipment and one journal recommended they should consist of: 2 two-gallon canvas bags of water, 4 half-pound cans of meat or fish, 4 one-pound packs of hard-tack, 2 pounds of sweet chocolate, 2 cans of fruit, personal effects and toiletries.

This load was designed to meet the needs of four people, but it does reflect the isolation of the traveller once he had left the safety of the city.

Speed limits were enforced during these pioneer days. Most, up to the First World War, were around 13 km/h (8 mph) in towns and 24 km/h (15 mph) in rural areas, with Wisconsin, Minnesota and Michigan as exceptions, where a daring 40 km/h (25 mph) was permitted under most circumstances.

Slowly the roads improved. There were some two million miles of connecting highways to be built; it is hard to imagine the magnitude of the programme. Carl Fisher, a man not given to half measures, wanted to promote a coast-to-coast road across the continent. He eventually succeeded, after much hindrance from Henry Ford and some fortunate help from who-

ever suggested that it should be called the Lincoln Memorial Highway. That happy choice of name attracted a great deal of supporting cash, mainly from towns who wished to be on a route with such a distinguished title. New York, Jersey City, Trenton, Pittsburgh, Fort Wayne, South Bend, Chicago Heights, Joliet, Clinton, Cedar Rapids, Council Bluffs, Omaha, Denver, Cheyenne, Salt Lake City, Reno, Sacramento, Oakland and San Francisco found themselves part of the Lincoln Highway. That most of these names are now known over much of the world is testimony to the business acumen of the city fathers who invested in the project. It was completed in the early 1920s.

The Lincoln Highway was only the start of a programme of bigger and better roads, and today the United States has some of the finest and most sophisticated in the world. It also has just a few of the worst, which is not surprising in view of the fact that the original undertaking was to surface roads which could have girdled the equator forty times.

THE ROARING TWENTIES

On 17 January 1920, the Eighteenth Amendment of the Constitution of the United States banning the sale and consumption of alcoholic liquor went into effect. Within an hour the first theft of liquor during America's 14-year prohibition period had taken place. These were the times "when every beer truck had its own tail gunner." Indeed, the gangster cars of the 1920's – vast Lincolns, Packards and Cadillacs with their gun

ports (touring cars were preferred because the arc of fire was less restricted) – were in a sense the essence of American motoring after the 1914–18 war; but the future was with the law-abiding motorists of the still-growing country.

The Dodge brothers were of the work-a-day world of transport with their auto parts business that at first had depended heavily on orders from Ford. They had even invested in Ford shares, initially buying 50 each. By 1914 Horace and John Dodge had abandoned the spare parts business, sued Ford for some $19 million in dividends (later profiting by $25 million for the sale of their shares), and had started to produce their own automobile, an extremely plain four-cylinder touring car of modest dimensions.

However, such had been the reputation of the company for high quality parts that an incredible 22,000 firms applied for Dodge dealerships. Within one short year Dodge ranked as the eighth largest car producer in the U.S.A. and by 1920 only Ford was ahead. In 1923 Dodge brought out the world's first closed sedan with an all-steel body, and in 1928 offered a six-cylinder model built on the same principle. At about this time, Walter Chrysler bought the Dodge Company for $175 million in a bid to out-power Ford and General Motors, the other two American giants.

Chrysler himself had not long been in the business with a product of his own name. In 1924, his first car – a plain sedan – had first been seen in New York. Its claims were considerable: a new, six cylinder, high compression engine, never offered

on a medium-priced car before. The American public showed its appreciation by ordering 32,000 in the first year. This was particularly gratifying for Walter Chrysler since he had not been allowed to exhibit the car in the New York Motor Show that year. Instead, he hired the lobby of the Commodore Hotel, in which most of the important show visitors were staying, and displayed it there.

The energetic railroad apprentice from Ellis, Kansas, also offered the public two other new models that year, the Plymouth Four and the De Soto Six, cars designed to fill several gaps in the market. But the Wall Street crash was only months away. This took America's car industry into its fourth phase. None but the fittest survived. Dozens of small companies disappeared overnight, some of which – such as Moon, Kissel, Gardner and Jordan – left the world less colourful.

Marmon, who tried to combat the depression with a one-model policy, also failed, but, like Reo, changed to truck manufacture. Peerless, after a last bid in the motor market with a fine all-aluminium car, also failed, and went into brewing as the Peerless Corporation in January 1934. Their product is today familiar to many as Carling.

Out of the Depression came America's five giants: Ford, General Motors, Chrysler, Packard and Nash, scarred but powerful, with almost all their small rivals dead. Some survived for a while, but the Depression outlasted most; production did not climb back to the 1928 figure of 3.8 million for ten long years. The last years of the Depression saw the failure of such names as Auburn, Stutz and Cord.

As in several other countries, the unemployment caused by the Depression was turned to advantage by using labour to extend the continent's road network. This, and a growing awareness of traffic flow and parking problems, helped create the motoring standards Americans know today. Moreover, American cars of the 1930s were to become renowned for rugged, long-lasting qualities, unlike their descendants of the 1950s. Europe, by contrast, was producing vehicles that had gadgets, gimmicks and simplicity of operation designed for the new mass-market of middle class motorists.

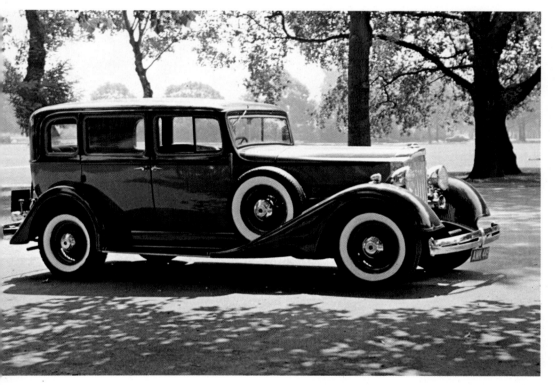

ABOVE: A Packard sedan, 1932. Leaders in the American luxury market, Packard had in 1932, just completed development of their new straight eight cylinder unit which had improved manifolds, higher compression and increased power output. Rival companies, Cadillac, Lincoln and Pierce-Arrow incorporated several Packard innovations at this time.

LEFT: Quality heavyweight: 1929 Pierce-Arrow. In 1928 the company had been placed under the control of the Studebaker Corporation and this new model was offered to the public. It housed a straight-eight engine under its massive hood and was a best-seller, giving the company its best-ever year.

RIGHT: Walter Chrysler, former farm boy and railroad mechanic had built his own empire by the time this 1926 "70" appeared. Production had jumped to 1,250 cars a day, lifting the young corporation to sixth place among all American motor manufacturers.

The Edwardians

The so-called Edwardian period opened on 22 January 1901 when Queen Victoria died. At the bedside was her eldest son, Albert Edward, Prince of Wales, already nearly sixty – a short, guttural-voiced man, horse lover, pioneer motorist, ladies man still, and now King.

His subjects put the 19th century firmly into the past and resolutely looked forward to the bright future, a Pandora's box of new delights. The social conventions (at least within the still rigidly defined classes) had loosened if not disappeared; discoveries such as flight, radio communication and cinematography were on the horizon. Medical science was promising near-eternal life, Britain was richer than ever. The young were about to enjoy a long golden summer of pleasure.

It was a tidy situation, a clean cut with Victorian ways, a new century, and happily, motoring fitted in with the atmosphere of progress – even in England, where the 1896 Act had released automobilists from the pedestrian pace of six and a half km/h (four mph). The fact that the new king was a motor enthusiast was also a help.

France was at this time ahead of the field; by 1901, its motor industry was ten years old with Panhard (established 1889), Peugeot (1889), Bollée (first production car 1896), Darracq (1896), Mors (1895), Delahaye and numerous others making motor cars for Europe. Even Germany had lagged behind the energetic French so much that the "official" language of motoring was not German but, as in fencing, French.

Britain, however, was catching up quickly. In 1903, compulsory registration of vehicles was introduced, along with motoring regulations reminiscent of today's. They stated the penalties for various misdemeanours such as "reckless or careless driving," or forging a licence. At the end of the 1903 Act a small but vital paragraph declared that: "*A person shall not, under any circumstances, drive a motor car on the public highway at a speed exceeding 20 miles an hour.*" This virtually released the brakes on early motoring. Financiers and manufacturers now saw that the people and the government had realized – at last – that motoring had arrived, and the hitherto stunted British motor industry slipped into high gear. It seemed that the small coterie of early motorists – Edge, Scott-Montagu, the Harmsworth family, Jarrott, Rolls and of course King Edward himself – had managed to persuade the government through pressures unrevealed to the public to move into the 20th century along with the rest of the developed world.

By 1906 Britain was producing cars with household names, even though some have since vanished – Austin, Wolseley, Riley, AC, Rover, Vauxhall, Humber and many that are rarely seen now except at veteran car assemblies, like Alldays, Deasy and Thornycroft. In 1906, Rolls-Royce were about to produce the Silver Ghost. A Rolls-Royce brochure of 1905 told the Edwardian upper classes in typically Edwardian terms of the virtues of the motor car from Manchester. "In consequence of the number of enquiries received by C. S. Rolls & Co.," it ran, "and the constant pressure brought to bear on them to produce in this country a motor vehicle of the VERY HIGHEST GRADE, which will compare favourably with the best continental makes, they have after much experiment perfected and placed upon the market AN ALL-BRITISH CAR. In its design has been incorporated what experience has proved to be the best features in the leading types of car, and to these have been added notable and most valuable improvements.

"The vehicle which C. S. Rolls & Co. now place before the public has been declared by experts to mark the MOST ADVANCE that has been made of late years in the brief history of Automobilism."

Then the brochure listed its ten, fifteen, twenty and thirty horsepower cars. The small one, with a Barker tonneau body (i.e. four-seater, rear passenger entrance, and open to the elements) cost £395; the 30 hp model (with a Barker six-seater limousine body) cost the magic figure of £1,000 precisely, and it was announced in addition that this model would run "from five to fifty five miles an hour without changing gear."

At this time the changing of gears was a hazardous and dreaded operation that needed the skill of a surgeon. The leather clutch, usually cone shaped, was often extremely fierce and could propel a car on engagement forward like a Grand Prix racer for the first few yards, jerking the driver almost into the back seats and leaving a trail of flying grit, or sparks if the tyres were steel studded. What happened during those uncontrolled moments was the basis of many a hair-raising story around the dinner table.

Although Rolls, Napier and some others had produced sixes for several years, until about 1905 the buyer's choice was usually between a one, two, or four cylinder engine – but now more variety was available from France, Germany and later from Italy. Money naturally dictated the type of car and what it offered.

There was a flourishing second-hand trade, which brought cars within the reach of the small merchant or modest professional, but not yet of the man in the street.

PREVIOUS PAGES: Engineer Ralph Lucas built his first experimental Valveless cars in 1901. The most successful was a two-stroke with twin vertical water-cooled cylinders mounted midships in the car. Later models were more conventional in layout and appearance. This is a 1914 Valveless.

RIGHT: By 1901 the F.I.A.T. organisation (the capitals were dropped in 1906) was making this 8 hp car, its fourth production model and the first to have its engine in front. Its two cylinder unit could bowl it along at a respectable 50 km/h (30 mph), a speed which at first created some cooling problems that were solved by using a honeycomb radiator.

Some of the advertisements of the day were surprisingly modern by mid-Edwardian times. Gone were the notices directed solely at the nobility and the gentry like this example from 1896: "This novel vehicle is propelled by an INTERNAL COMBUSTION engine of two cylinders and six horsepower, relying on petroleum spirit for its motive power and will attain the comfortable speed of 12 miles an hour on the level ground." Long gone also were the days when you fixed a notice on your car when you left it, informing admiring spectators that "This is an autocar, some people call it a motor car. It is worked by a petroleum motor, the motor is of four horse power. It will run sixty miles on one charge of oil. No, it can't explode, there is no boiler."

That sort of public relations was useful before the British public had been given the chance to see cars in plenty during the great Thousand Mile Trial in 1900. This was a round-Britain run that brought the car to the people by exhibiting scores of them in halls up and down the country. Now that people were familiar with cars, however, the advertisement could assume a degree of knowledge:

"Wanted: good reliable car with horizontal engine, nine or ten hp, chain drive, two ignitions preferred. M.O.I. valves, well lubricated and cooled. Must be cheap. Mansfield, Church Street, Ashby-de-la-Zouche."

An offer of sale would have been like this:

"*Daimler* – Gentleman having bought a 45 hp Daimler has his 28–36 hp for sale ... in perfect order fitted with electric and magneto ignitions, three electric lamps, two large headlamps, glass screen, numerous spares, six inner tubes and one new

LEFT: An Opel 10/18 double phaeton of 1909 – elegance from Rüsselsheim in Germany, typical of the Edwardian period of motoring.

ABOVE RIGHT: Baby Peugeot 1902. With a single cylinder motor this little "one-lunger" had three forward speeds and was shaft driven.

RIGHT: This 40 hp Austin York Landaulette was a favourite for a drive in the park with Edwardian ladies. The car had a vast amount of headroom, a feature often insisted upon by Herbert Austin who, it was said, never travelled anywhere without his bowler hat firmly on his head.

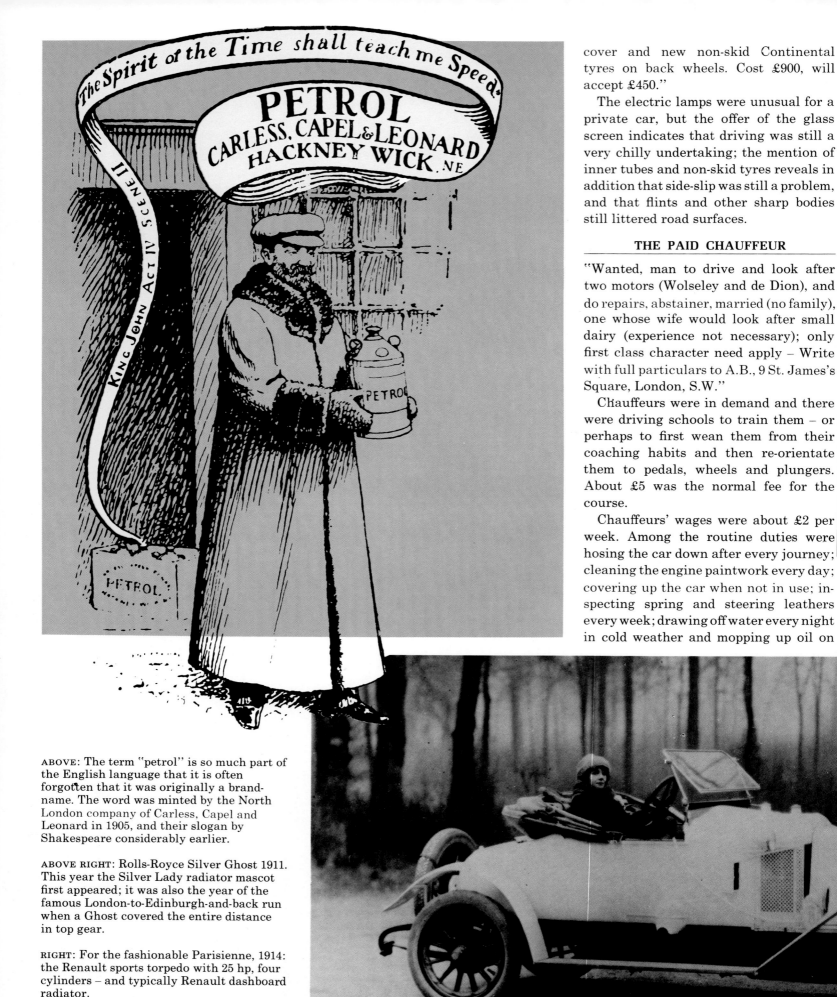

The Spirit of the Time shall teach me Speed.

KING JOHN ACT IV SCENE II

PETROL
CARLESS, CAPEL & LEONARD
HACKNEY WICK. N E

PETROL

PETROL

cover and new non-skid Continental tyres on back wheels. Cost £900, will accept £450."

The electric lamps were unusual for a private car, but the offer of the glass screen indicates that driving was still a very chilly undertaking; the mention of inner tubes and non-skid tyres reveals in addition that side-slip was still a problem, and that flints and other sharp bodies still littered road surfaces.

THE PAID CHAUFFEUR

"Wanted, man to drive and look after two motors (Wolseley and de Dion), and do repairs, abstainer, married (no family), one whose wife would look after small dairy (experience not necessary); only first class character need apply – Write with full particulars to A.B., 9 St. James's Square, London, S.W."

Chauffeurs were in demand and there were driving schools to train them – or perhaps to first wean them from their coaching habits and then re-orientate them to pedals, wheels and plungers. About £5 was the normal fee for the course.

Chauffeurs' wages were about £2 per week. Among the routine duties were hosing the car down after every journey; cleaning the engine paintwork every day; covering up the car when not in use; inspecting spring and steering leathers every week; drawing off water every night in cold weather and mopping up oil on

ABOVE: The term "petrol" is so much part of the English language that it is often forgotten that it was originally a brand-name. The word was minted by the North London company of Carless, Capel and Leonard in 1905, and their slogan by Shakespeare considerably earlier.

ABOVE RIGHT: Rolls-Royce Silver Ghost 1911. This year the Silver Lady radiator mascot first appeared; it was also the year of the famous London-to-Edinburgh-and-back run when a Ghost covered the entire distance in top gear.

RIGHT: For the fashionable Parisienne, 1914: the Renault sports torpedo with 25 hp, four cylinders – and typically Renault dashboard radiator.

the floor at all times. Chauffeurs were particularly discouraged from racing the engine under the pretence of adjustment.

Some chauffeurs did indeed have to be watched closely; some of the complaints by long-suffering masters have rung true over the years. Their mechanical ability was often non-existent. Stories of reckless driving are endless: "I remember a huge Dane who drove me to the station in the North of England who, having charged into a bank with the car, by way of explanation said, 'You haf never been so near to be dead as you was this night.' "

An early 20th century chauffeur would be out in all weathers with no more shelter against the storm than a coachman of a hundred years earlier. Even towards the end of the pre-first war period, when motor cars became more enclosed, the driver was often left out in the cold by the designer.

EARLY MOTORISTS AND THE LAW

If there was a constant war of nerves between owner and chauffeur, there was certainly open battle between the motorist and the police during much of the Edwardian period. The old school of magistrate, accustomed to forelock-tugging penitents, was much put out by the new "criminal" appearing before him. Motorists, almost always of the same class as the magistrate, incurred heavy fines from the old school of horse-loving law dispensers.

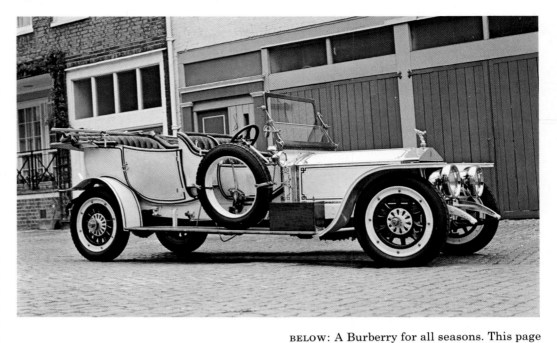

BELOW: A Burberry for all seasons. This page from the Burberry catalogue of early Edwardian days shows sensible wear for the open vehicles of the time. The victoria, which the owner is driving as if it were a tram, predates the occupants' dress style by a year or two.

Screened by the wayside chestnut tree
The village P.C. stands.
The "cop" a crafty man is he
With a stop watch in his hands
And the muscles of his lower jaw
Are set like iron bands.

He goes each morning to his lair
And hides among the trees,
He hears the sound of motors there
And sets his mind at ease,
For it seems to tell of captives – and
Promotions follows These!

Hiding and clocking, summoning,
Onward through life he goes:
Each night he's had his vengeance on
Some of his scorching foes.
Somebody summoned, somebody "done"
Has earned a night's repose.

It is not surprising that this little ditty
was published anonymously in *The Motor*
during 1904, for this was certainly the
situation between motorist and con-
stabulary over most of England. The time
had come for drivers to act in their own
defence.

Two prominent motorists, the racing
driver Charles Jarrott and his friend
William Letts, set up a cycle patrol on the
London to Brighton road to warn motorists of speed traps, forming their own
organization – the Automobile Association. People flocked to join, particularly
when they were told that they would be
defended in court by the Association.

Scouts arranged signs on the roads to
warn their members of speed traps, or

signalled them down. A few went to jail
for it. Then the AA had the bright idea
of *not* saluting members when there was
danger ahead. "When a patrol does not
salute," ran the advice, "STOP and ask
the reason." The motorist would then be
given a private warning about the local
trap.

In time, animosity between driver and
the police waned. The motor car had
arrived permanently – there were some
100,000 on the roads of Britain by 1910,
and the AA grew from a cheeky pressure
group into a respectable body.

The Edwardian period in Europe was
a time of refinement rather than innovation for the motor car. Styles such as gig,
dog-cart and dos-à-dos had disappeared
from the brochures and been replaced by
saloon, tourer and torpedo, some of which
were to last into the late Twenties, and
some until today. At first tourers, with
their so-called all-weather protection,
comprised the first move towards the enclosed car. Sunbeam, Austin, Calthorpe,
Vauxhall, Rover and Riley were the prin-
cipal makers of canvas-covered tourers,
although before bringing out the Seven
Austin seemed to favour the tall walk-
through limousine or town car with
chamfered glass and rigid roof. Two or
three years before the 1914–18 war, the
clean-lined torpedo shape began to evolve
– the 1912 Swedish Scania-Vabis was a
good example and the 1913–14 Sunbeam
came close.

Meanwhile, the German motor industry was progressing. Adler, a founder

member, had built a shaft-drive car almost as early as Louis Renault and were
now making tourers with units ranging
from 1.3 to 9 litres, as were Daimler and
Benz in the larger, luxury range.

French companies, now more numerous
than ever before or since, were led, in
quantity at least, by Renault, who in 1907
were selling some 3,000 cars a year. They
were also taking action against manufacturers in other countries who were
making direct copies of their models. In
1908 the first Renault six cylinder car
appeared. Louis Renault, now recognized
leader of the French motor industry, had
been made a *Chevalier de la Légion
d'Honneur* in 1906, for "Boldness of design, independence of spirit, knowledge
of his time, its needs and its potential, and
the prodigious capacity for work that
made him a captain of industry."

Before those golden days ended so
abruptly in war, defence ministries had
been closely observing the motor industry
and its products, and rejected the car as a
weapon. It was thought staff cars were
useful enough; but it took an emergency
at the battle of the Marne in 1914 to alert
military thinkers to the car's potential. A
fleet of 600 Renault *"Deux Pattes"* (two
cylinder) taxis from Paris rushed relief
troops to the front. From then on, warfare
became mechanized.

France's *Belle Epoque* was generally a
time of improvement and refinement. Its
last products provided basic designs upon
which the cars of the Twenties were built,
the cars of the vintage years.

ABOVE: Twenty two cars were entered in the 1907 Tourist Trophy race at the Isle of Man. Only two finished. The winner was a 20 hp Rover 3.5 litre driven by Ernest Courtis at an average speed of 46.3 km/h (28.8 mph). This is a Rover 20 of the same date.

ABOVE LEFT: Edwardian driver's-eye view – from the seat of a 1909 Alldays tourer, a vehicle of four cylinders, 14 hp and great dignity.

BELOW LEFT: This 1913 Morgan was made when the Malvern-based Morgan Motor Company was three years old. By the end of 1913 the 1,100 cc Morgan had gained more awards for reliability and speed than any other light car or cycle-car.

FAR LEFT: Built from 1906 to 1913, this Austin Endcliffe tourer was a popular car in the days when motorists would lay up their vehicles for the winter. This example, posed against a background of a slightly later date, housed a 4.4 litre side-valve engine.

RIGHT: Fundamental motoring for a modest price could have been the Trojan slogan. This is a 1912 prototype; commercial production began in 1922.

THE 20's

Prosperity, which the advent of peace in 1918 seems to have promised for all, proved in reality exasperatingly elusive. The gaiety and ease of the Twenties, with "bright young things", tennis parties and country house week-ends, were only a part of the picture; the world war was bound to bring about some stern social changes.

Nevertheless, car manufacturers' prospects in 1919 were distinctly bright. There was a world shortage of motor cars – indeed of motor vehicles of every kind – due both to the concentration of the war production over the previous four years and the destruction which the war itself had wrought. Not only that, the emancipation of ordinary men and women – which was the inevitable result of their years of war service – created a demand for private transport which had scarcely existed in 1913.

There was, of course, a large amount of war surplus material salvaged from the battlefields of Europe and much of it was perfectly suitable for conversion to civilian use. The allied governments of France, Britain and America appropriated large numbers of such cars, trucks and motor cycles and repatriated them. Some were sold in government sales (in Britain from a large dump at Slough) but they were essentially an embarrassment to governments who had lately been at war and were now trying to stimulate peacetime economy. Every war surplus vehicle sold at a knock-down price meant one less new vehicle sold by the manufacturer and so, while the public fumed at the shortages and the delays in new deliveries, perfectly good ex-military vehicles rotted in bonded compounds, as the authorities endeavoured to encourage the sales of new vehicles.

America was in a far better position for recovery than most, having maintained production of cars throughout the war with barely the suggestion of a pause even during direct involvement in 1917–18. While her cheaper cars were crude by European standards, mass production had made them utterly reliable, easy to maintain and cheap, and many now seeking their first cars had learned to drive on an American vehicle during the war.

Peacetime brought production problems. There were shortages of raw materials; installations and machinery had been either worn out or damaged during the war years, workers were more militant and the revolt against the old ruling class which had started in the trenches resulted in labour disputes and strikes in all sections of industry.

On the other hand, firms which had previously had little to do with motor manufacture found themselves after the armistice with factories hugely expanded by the war effort and with no more military orders. They turned to the manufacture of motor cars and other vehicles, and never before or since were there so many new firms offering such a wide choice. London companies like Kingsbury Engineering and Storey turned from munitions to motor manufacture; famous aviation firms like Short, Sopwith and Graham-White found that their military aircraft order books had emptied overnight and using names such as A.B.C., Short Ashby, G.W. (all light cars for the new British buyer), they fought to survive in a fresh field where competition was fierce from the beginning.

PREVIOUS PAGES: During the Twenties, Humber of Britain produced solid and reliable family cars, eschewing the world of sporting competition. This two litre two seater made in 1927 was a slightly less conservative example.

LEFT: André Citroën had made munitions during the First World War, and when it ended needed a new product to occupy his machines. The result – the 10 hp Type A of 1919, first of the Citroën line.

BELOW LEFT: Steam was fighting a rearguard action in the struggle against the internal combustion engine, and although the steam car was dead in Europe by 1900, the Americans staged a late come-back. It was unsuccessful, and this 1920 model was one of the last to emerge from the Stanley works, although the company remained in business until 1927.

BELOW: This was the period when the most recognizable feature of the car was often its radiator. It was logical that many advertisements of the time should feature it.

La Voiture de l'Elite   103, Av.ue de Villiers

Rickenbacker
A · CAR · WORTHY · OF · ITS · NAME

THE outstanding characteristic of any 8 cylinder motor is acceleration. We point with pride to the Rickenbacker performance on that score.

FOR magical action, and an exquisite sensation, a free flowing, abundant, unhampered power, you will find the Rickenbacker 8 a joy to drive.

Famous "Six" Prices		Vertical "Eight" Prices	
Sport Phaeton - - $1595		Sport Phaeton - - $2195	
Coupe - - - 2095	f. o. b. Detroit —	Coupe - - - 2695	
Sedan - - - 2195	plus war tax	Sedan - - - 2795	

RICKENBACKER MOTOR COMPANY
DETROIT, MICHIGAN

encouraged some of the shrewdest entrepreneurs, largely to the detriment of the higher quality automobile. Of the large manufacturers who used the method, Morris Motors were one of the most successful, and Clyno (who foolishly chose to operate a price war against the Oxford company) was typical of those who failed. W. R. Morris's Cowley and Oxford models elevated production figures in Britain to unprecedented heights, enabling him to buy up his major suppliers one by one and eventually to become a manufacturer in his own right.

LEFT: Captain Eddie Rickenbacker was well-known as an air ace and racing driver. Built from 1922 until 1927, Rickenbacker cars were among the best of the smaller American independents.

RIGHT: The Perry was made by former Birmingham cyclemakers in small numbers. Their 1913 sports model, with raked steering wheel, 875 cc unit and 3-speed gearbox, had claimed top speed of nearly 60 km/h (40 mph). The company was bought in 1919 by A. Harper and Bean Limited, who re-designed it and called it the Bean.

BELOW: For the travelling worker? Perhaps for the professional man or the inspector, as the text of this 1926 advertisement says. The Model T was still being made at this date and the very much more advanced Model A was still two years away.

THE AMERICAN INFLUENCE

American vehicles represented a threat to European and British motor sales, and in an effort to limit imports many countries, including Britain, imposed heavy duties on American cars. Despite this, the period up until 1941 saw an increasing influence of American design, even in France and Germany where American cars did not sell as well as in Britain.

While makers such as Ford, Dodge and Chevrolet set the trend and the records in production figures, other specialist American firms like Duesenberg, whose luxury "straight eight" (eight cylinders in a line) was introduced in 1920, and Templar, who concentrated on high-class light cars, competed in the United States and overseas alongside established purveyors to the carriage trade like Peerless, Packard, Pierce-Arrow and Locomobile.

In the American middle-market the struggle was, if anything, as desperate as in the economy price bracket, since it encompassed a great many long-established and conservative companies, like for example Apperson, who had existed happily on an annual production of about 3,000 units before the war, but now lacked the capital or the facilities to compete with rivals like Hudson, who in 1920 produced 46,000 units. The solution adopted by many was simply to stop manufacturing their own major components, and to buy these in from specialist manufacturers. This transition from manufacture to assembly marked the beginning of the end for many firms, and opened the market to a great many new companies whose only claim to fame was that they could successfully bolt together other people's work.

This "scissors and paste" mentality created some of the dullest motor cars and

For the Travelling Worker

FOR the professional man or inspector whose work takes him abroad in all weathers, the Ford Coupé is the finest possible combination of economy and weathertight comfort.

Its handsome all-steel body—strong and rattle-proof —in rich colours, its low deep seats and balloon tyres, make it a car of refinement, and yet it has all the old reliability that has sold thirteen million Fords to the World.

It is a busy car for busy men—a tireless worker—the finest possible investment for the outdoor man to whom time is money. See it at your Authorised Ford Dealer's.

£170 net (AT WORKS, MANCHESTER)

THE MOTORIST

The motorist of the 1920s was probably better served in terms of choice, quality and value for money than ever before or since – particularly during the years 1924–7. A whole new generation of motorists, most of them ex-servicemen and women, took to the road and reaped the benefits which four years of concentrated war production had bestowed upon the technology of mass production, metallurgy and mechanical efficiency – particularly in the small car which now became more readily available.

This new four-wheeled army both demanded and paid for a crash programme of road improvement which was long overdue, particularly in America, and the whole concept of the motor vehicle as a means of improving the life of the individual and his family was extended from the upper classes to the man in the street, with far-reaching social consequences.

Industrial strife apart, the Twenties were dominated by a spirit of optimism, both national and individual, largely a natural reaction to ending the horrors of war. The social and domestic life was influenced increasingly by women, who had demonstrated their equality most convincingly at the wheels of ambulances and buses and in the munitions factories. This newly acknowledged emancipation, accompanied by brashness and inelegance, served only to emphasize that the long Edwardian summer was indeed over.

Acknowledging the power which women now wielded, manufacturers offered a variety of open and closed body cars aimed directly at the woman driver,

LEFT: Artist Fouqueray implies that service stations were few and far between during the Twenties.

with a range of colour schemes previously unheard of. The dress revolution, which had started when Cadillac standardized the electric self-starter in 1912, still went on: since an elaborate *coiffure* is scarcely practical in an open two-seater, the Eton crop and semi-shingle came into fashion. Outdoor life, the open road, adventure, travel, sport and other healthy activities were heavily promoted through motor advertisements of the day and succeeded in establishing the myth that the 1920s were one long summer holiday.

Ford's mainstay, the ubiquitous and eccentric Model T, went from strength to strength during the Twenties, with a peak of 1,817,891 cars produced in 1923 in America alone. Ford himself was an outdoor man, and did much to promote agriculture and outdoor activities like

camping and touring, and tourists certainly dominated the roads of America, Britain and Europe for the first five years of the decade. In Britain particularly, clubs sprang up all over the country organizing rallies and hill climbs. Semi-sporting events and those which catered for individual makes of car were supported vigorously by the manufacturers, all of whom were anxious to promote marque loyalty. During this period most major manufacturers produced a house magazine aimed at both dealers and customers.

FROM FAST TOURER TO CHEAP SALOON

From the tourer developed the fast tourer (now usually called a sports car) and although America offered open cars with sporting specifications like the assembled

Gordon Playboy, and some out-and-out racers, of which the Mercer and the Stutz were examples, the fast tourer remained essentially the province of British and French makers.

Of these, the Bentley has now acquired an almost immortal reputation, but Lagonda and the now little-remembered Reading firm of H.E. both produced notable specimens. France had its Chenard-Walcker, Delage, Ballot, Hispano-Suiza and numerous others, mostly characterized by a more feminine ambience than the brute force of, say, a Bentley. Ettore Bugatti, whose own cars were sculpted rather than engineered, is credited with a most apt description of the Bentley. He called it *"le camion le plus vite du monde"* – "the fastest lorry in the world."

The fast tourer and the small French

ABOVE: In 1919 Hispano-Suiza produced the H6B, a car that was so far ahead of its contemporaries that it could be said to have set the standard for the vintage years. The 37 hp 6.6-litre ohc engine was in fact one bank of a wartime V12 aero-engine. Seen here is a smaller-engined 1928–9 Barcelona. In the background, an all-weather-bodied Silver Ghost Rolls-Royce.

RIGHT: The enormous six cylinder "45" of 1924 was not typical of Renault's production. Its 9.1-litre engine contrasted sharply with the little 6 hp KJ type of 1923 with which Louis Renault hoped to stem Citroën's rising sales, but nevertheless it remained available until 1928.

BELOW: Britain produced a number of high quality manufactured (rather than "assembled") light cars immediately before and after the First War, and the Calcott from Coventry – like its Birmingham neighbour the Calthorpe – was one of the best. This is the 11.9 hp model of 1923, made just three years before Singer took over the company.

ABOVE: If Herbert Austin's "Seven" had not made its appearance in 1922 the Rover "Eight" might well have been the most successful light car of the 1920's. Equipped with a transverse-mounted horizontal air-cooled twin-cylinder engine, it relied upon air scoops on either side of the bonnet to aid cooling.

LEFT: The image of fast and expensive sporting activities was used more frequently in promotional material when it was discovered by the ad-agents that the exclusivity theme rubbed off onto the product.

sportscar were achieving a specialized following, but the cheap, all-steel body pioneered by firms like Dodge in America and Citroën in France was to be the death of the open family tourer. The arrival of the Essex "coach" (two-door saloon) in 1922 hastened this transition, and by the late Twenties the public was beginning to forsake draughts, inefficient hoods and sidescreens for the comfort of the saloon and closed coupé.

MASS MARKET

If Britain ever came close to producing its own version of the Model T Ford (Ford's assembly plant at Manchester made cars based on the American design) it was the Trojan. Designed in 1910 by Leslie Hounsfield, and put into production by Leyland in 1922 after they had failed with their luxury Leyland Eight, it was probably the most bizarre design ever to be mass-produced. "It's weird, but it goes," said Housefield to the Leyland Board – and they were persuaded.

Uncompromisingly spartan, virtually everything about the Trojan flew in the face of established manufacturing practice. It used solid tyres allied to enormous cantilever "wondersprings" front and rear; its two stroke, four cylinder engine lived horizontally under the floor; it employed a two-speed epi-

cyclic gearbox (like the Model T) and it drove its rear axle by exposed chain. Such a combination, all hung on a deep "baking tin" chassis, added up to a cheap, reliable, slow, ugly car. It sold at the healthy rate of up to 85 units a week during the height of its popularity. Garages hated it, and not a few displayed signs saying "No Trojans".

The Trojan, beloved of impecunious clergymen and commercial travellers, was the only car ever advertised in the *Church Times* and in 1925 became the cheapest all-British car at £125. Its ability to slog up the steepest hills earned

TOP LEFT: This 1922 Bullnose Morris Oxford used a continental-designed Hotchkiss side-valve engine of 1.8 litres.

ABOVE: Towards the end of the Model T's life Henry Ford eventually conceded that it would have to be made more attractive. This model, the Tudor (two-door) sports a nickelled radiator shell.

TOP RIGHT: A 1924 Trojan. It had 10 hp under the bonnet delivered by a noisy two-stroke horizontally-mounted underfloor engine, and solid tyres plus enormous "wondersprings".

RIGHT: This 1923 Austin Seven was a real car in miniature, with a four cylinder water-cooled engine and shaft drive. It was utterly reliable.

it a following in sporting hill climb events and its agricultural specification did not deter Brooke Bond Tea, the Grooms Bread Company and others from maintaining large fleets of the van version, which were still in service until the early Fifties. Even the R.A.F. favoured it for tender work.

THE AUSTIN SEVEN

"It is a decent car for the man who, at present, can only afford a motor cycle and sidecar, and yet has the ambition to become a motorist." Sir Herbert Austin. To Austin's board of directors, the proposal by Sir Herbert Austin to build an ultra-light car seemed madness, and its enthusiasm was scarcely lukewarm. The company was doing badly, indeed had passed through a period of near bankruptcy, and the tiny bath tub with the pram hood designed on Austin's billiard table in secret seemed hardly the salvation so desperately needed.

The board was wrong. The "baby" Austin Seven sold prodigiously, remained in production for over 16 years with only improvements of details, saved the Austin company, and put over 200,000 new

motorists on the road. Not only that, but it was received by the public with an eagerness which immediately convinced Austin that he had made the correct decision – even though the Press joked at the car's diminutive size. "Business men can keep clean in them," ran the brochure: "Ideal for women who can change speed with ease," claimed the advertisements. "Get one for each foot," or "if you've run out of petrol, you'll need a new flint" quipped the wits. But when the public saw the photographs of the Austin Seven's

bulky creator at the wheel, with his bowler crammed squarely down on his head, they bought. With father at the wheel, wife in the tiny bucket seat alongside and the children in the back, off they went to the seaside for the day – thousands and thousands of people who had never had the chance before.

The 30's
A Time of Reckoning

It is very easy to condemn the period from 1930 to the outbreak of the second world war as that in which coach-built composite bodywork gave way to steel pressing. Handbuilt motor cars were replaced by characterless mass-produced vehicles, and the functionally aesthetic car of the 1920s gave way to a less elegant machine. This may well be, but there were many reasons, evolutionary and economic, for the decline in quality. And one reason was the growth in mass demand. Many people could at last afford the deposit on a modest vehicle, one that could take the family out for a spin in the country on a Sunday afternoon.

While the 1920s had served as an introduction to motoring for many, the following decade was the period during which car ownership became commonplace, and sad though it may have been for diehard motoring enthusiasts to contemplate, the average motorist did not insist on, and often knew nothing about, cornering ability, rapid acceleration, and a stable and exhilarating top speed. Then, as now, the family motorist looked for reliability, simplicity, low initial cost, low-cost running, and some comfort.

After a decade of coping with unfathomable breakdowns, punctures, draughts and all-weather equipment which wasn't, the man in the street represented a body of opinion which the motor car manufacturer ignored only at his peril. The early years of the Thirties were held in the grip of a world trade depression, and competition for customers was fierce. The man who could afford any kind of motor car was in a position to demand what he considered an uncommonly good bargain.

The years from 1929 until 1934 were unkind to the motor industry, and a great many names which had once been considered giants of the industry vanished, sometimes almost overnight. Even larger firms were not left unscathed – Studebaker, Nash and Willys in America all suffered periods of near-bankruptcy; Standard of Coventry were saved only by their little fabric-saloon Nine; Swift succumbed in the same city in 1931, and Ford's American production figures plummeted from 1,155,162 in 1930 to less than half this figure in 1931 – to give Chevrolet leading place in the sales race for the first time, a position they were to hold (except in 1935) throughout the decade until America's entry into the war in 1941.

Hardest hit were the luxury and specialist producers. Even Rolls-Royce were forced to close down their factory at Springfield, Massachusetts, and Peerless, once with Packard and Pierce-Arrow considered America's finest cars, threw in the towel too. Germany's Daimler and Benz had amalgamated in the late Twenties for safety, and now it was Austro-Daimler's time to search for help. Their A.D.R., a beautiful eight cylinder car designed for the luxury life was their last great work before the company became Steyr-Daimler-Puch in 1934.

DEPRESSION AND BANKRUPTCY

In France, it might be thought that no one actually went bankrupt since the old aristocratic names tended, like the aristocracy itself in the face of a proletariat revolution, to band together either by mergers or, more commonly, by a cannibalistic arrangement whereby each supplied the other with components, factory space, personnel, and sometimes even cash. Thus we find Chenard-Walcker eking out an existence in association with Delahaye until 1932, then degenerating into a *pot pourri* of Citroën, Matford and a few of their own parts. Delage merged with Delahaye with the latter

PREVIOUS PAGES: In 1927 Henry Ford's factory came to a virtual standstill for six months while a replacement for the Model T was prepared. The result was the Model A of 1928, a conventional four cylinder engined car with four wheel brakes, which recaptured the sales lead from Chevrolet in 1929. This 1932 model was one of the last before the company began to concentrate on a new V8.

RIGHT: It has been said that Sir William Lyons never designed an ugly car, and certainly it is difficult to think of a Jaguar which did not please the eye. Before he commenced manufacture of his own cars, Lyons concentrated upon improving other people's products, and in addition to providing special bodies for Swift, Standard, and Fiat he designed this 1931 Swallow, based on an Austin Seven chassis.

BELOW LEFT: Throughout the 1930s Riley, independent until 1938, continued to build small-to-medium cars of high quality. This 1930 tourer relied upon the famous "nine" engine, designed by Hugh Rose for the 1926 Monaco model, with twin camshafts and high pushrods. It was a design which was to remain the basis of all Riley engines until 1957.

LEFT: Although it was not the first £100 car
to be offered by a large manufacturer
(William Morris' spartan little 8 hp open
Morris Minor of 1931 anticipated it) the
Ford "Y" saloon, introduced in 1933, was the
first successful model to achieve wide
acceptance – and was reduced to £100 in
October 1935. It was the first true British
Ford, although it was also made in Germany.
Its transverse springing was a reversion to
Model T practice.

company in control. De Lavaud rented factory space from La Buire, who in any event barely lasted into 1930. Georges Irat adopted front wheel drive and, later in 1939, Citroën's 11 CV engine too, the latter firm also supplying bodies to La Licorne in 1937 and 1938.

Even Gabriel Voisin, always an individualist, was forced to stand by and see the cars bearing his name using the American Graham 3½ litre engine in place of his beloved sleeve valve by 1937. When asked publicly why he had always persisted with his unusual bodywork and the sleeve valve engine design, he thought for a moment, and then in his characteristically blunt way answered "Because I was a damned fool!"

Arch-rivals Louis Renault and André Citroën – representing the establishment and the successful upstart respectively – fought a fierce commercial battle during this period, and Citroën, who had always

sent his new models round to the Renault works at Billancourt in a cock-a-snook attitude, lost. His personal extravagances, coupled with the expense of a brand new factory at Javel, finally broke him, and the banks whom he had always despised let him down badly. A few months before the introduction of the revolutionary 1934 *Traction Avant* Citroën, the car that was to popularize front wheel drive in Europe, André lost control of his company. Louis Renault was approached by the banks to take it

over but refused: "I could not do that to him," he said. Citroën never recovered from the blow and died in 1935, although his cars proved a resounding success and under new management the company survived.

Like Crossley in Britain and Reo in America, many firms – Luc Court, De Dion Bouton, and Unic among them – switched their emphasis, and eventually all their production, to commercial vehicles and thus survived the worst years.

The economic chaos and unemployment which the Depression brought with it had unexpected and in some cases far-reaching results. Roosevelt's New Deal put America on the road to recovery, while Britain found itself with a short-lived Labour Government under Ramsay MacDonald in 1929. In Italy Mussolini's ambition was to recreate the Roman Empire, and Hitler's was to build a state which would last a thousand years. Unfortunate though the events which these latter two ambitions were to bring about,

LEFT: Line-up on the grid for the start of a handicap race (some of the entries here are already showing their age) in the Thirties.

BELOW LEFT: Oulton Park Cheshire, 1972, looking very much as the grid must have appeared in about 1936, with a predominance of ERAs, the British cars that upheld the country's prestige in the voiturette category during the Thirties, when Britain scored few Grand Prix victories. Mainspring of the ERA project was Raymond Mays, who went on to organize and promote the BRM after the war.

BELOW: Artist Roy Nockolds captures the atmosphere of speed and contrast in this Brooklands poster of the Thirties.

BROOKLANDS
500 MILES RACE
SEPT. 24
STARTING at 11 A.M.

R.O. Nockolds.

THE WORLD'S FASTEST LONG DISTANCE RACE
Organised by THE BRITISH RACING DRIVERS' CLUB.
ADMISSION 3s. 6d. (including tax) CHILDREN 1s. 6d. (including tax)
DETAILS FROM:
THE BRITISH RACING DRIVERS' CLUB, Ltd., Bangalore House, Newton Street, W.C.2 (Holborn 0161), or
BROOKLANDS MOTOR COURSE, WEYBRIDGE, SURREY.
CHEAP COMBINED RAIL AND ADMISSION TICKETS FROM SOUTHERN RAILWAY STATIONS.
COVERED STANDS.

the immediate result was a tremendous boost for the motor industries of both their respective countries.

Heavily subsidized by the Nazi Government, racing teams headed by Mercedes-Benz and Auto Union dominated the circuits of Europe up until the outbreak of war in 1939, and to a lesser extent the pattern was repeated in Italy when Alfa Romeo passed into State ownership in 1933.

In Britain, perhaps least hit by the Depression despite heavy unemployment,

BELOW: On the right, the race-winning, trend-setting BMW 328, the two-seater sports car developed from the 1,971 cc Type 326 which had helped keep the company in the racing limelight. The power unit, producing 50 bhp in the 326, was by 1936, the year the Type 328 was introduced, a healthy 80 hp, giving the car a top speed of 160 km/h (100 mph). Two litre sports car racing became a BMW preserve for several years following the appearance of the now classic 328. The car on the left is a BMW 327, developed from the 328 and produced from 1937 to 1940.

TOP: The boat-tailed 1935 Auburn Speedster developed 150 bhp, and every one sold was guaranteed by the Auburn-Cord-Duesenberg combine to have been tested to a speed in excess of 160 km/h (100 mph).

ABOVE RIGHT: Dunlop put the world on rubber, and by the late 1930s were firmly established, with Michelin, as one of the leading tyre manufacturers. This dignified 1933 advertisement is designed to indicate to a discerning public that Dunlop is up there with the white tie and tails.

ABOVE LEFT: Packard Sedan 1931. This American quality company made power units of six, eight (the standard engine) and 12 cylinders – and when chief rival Cadillac brought out a V16 in 1930, matched them by 1934 with a similar engine, and independent suspension.

no such state sponsorship existed, and in the summer of 1931 the unthinkable happened when Bentley went broke. Napier, who had forsaken the luxury car market in 1924 in favour of aero engines made a bid for the company and many wished that it had been successful. It was not. Rolls-Royce gained control, production was transferred to Derby and thereafter the marque was little more than a Rolls-Royce in Bentley clothing. Although fast, it was too quiet and smooth to satisfy the followers of the earlier Cricklewood version.

However, the luxury market was an insecure business and it was the mass-producers of small to medium cars who were able to make the most of the economy-conscious atmosphere of the time. Austin and Morris consolidated the strong position they had built for themselves in the previous decade, Austin continuing the "Seven" and "Twelve-four" models and adding a "Ten" in 1932. Morris, lagging behind at the bottom end of the scale, and unsuccessful with their £100 "Minor" introduced in 1931, initially adopted the same policy as Singer and tended to fritter away their hard-won advantages by offering too many different models. However, the new Morris 8 saved the day in 1935 and by 1939 the Oxford company had built its first million cars.

It was a difficult time too for the builders of bespoke coachwork, and those who did not fade away completely survived by lowering their sights somewhat, and building commercial bodies or offering factory-approved long-run options on mundane middle-class chassis. Some of the prettiest drophead coupé and semi-sporting bodies appeared during this period on chassis ranging from Vauxhall to Humber and British Salmson to Invicta. In France the same phenomenon could be observed, although the Americans, dedicated to pressed steel and mass production, tended to steer clear of such customization on the cheaper production cars. The "woody" or station wagon was a later development born of the war-time and post-war steel shortage.

If the late Twenties saw a craze for the eight cylinder engine, the 1930's must be remembered as the era of the cheap small "six". At a time when everyone still had unpleasant memories of double de-clutching on the old "crash" type gearbox used during and before the Twenties, anything which made gear changing easier – particularly for women – tended to attract the buyers. Synchromesh was one

solution and the flexible small six was another. Unfortunately, putting a six cylinder engine into a "ten" horsepower chassis leaves very little room for a four-seater body, and almost without exception the results tended to be cramped. Some cars of sporting pretensions – like the Wolseley Hornet Special – did emerge, but generally these were scorned by real enthusiasts, for whom the M.G. Midget or Morgan, or a secondhand sports car from the previous decade, was a more exciting proposition.

Almost alone among newcomers who became successful during the period were Simca of France, who started operations in the moribund Donnet factory at Nanterre, manufacturing Fiats under licence. It is significant, however, that the year was 1934 and the worst of the Depression was over. Others tried hard and failed, and of these the De Vaux built in California and at Grand Rapids, Michigan from 1931–2 (and by Continental Motor Company of Detroit until 1934) deserved to succeed, but like Kaiser-Fraser after 1945, failed to beat the established Detroit giants at their own game.

GIMMICKS AND GADGETRY

It must not be thought, however, that the whole of the 1930s were fraught with financial gloom. After 1935 the world economic situation improved and the scene brightened considerably. A note of levity (in hindsight of course) was introduced into the motoring saga by the endless gadgetry with which manufacturers hoped to woo customers who were demanding higher standards of comfort. Very soon the prospective customer was faced with a confusing set of options including electric and manual pre-selector gear boxes, free-wheel devices, manual overdrives, and a wide variety of electric traffic indicators (some almost immediately declared illegal by the authorities and hastily withdrawn). Most of these refinements were given euphemistic names dreamed up by the advertising and sales departments, but very few of them survived for more than a season or two.

AUTOBAHN, BY-PASS AND FREEWAY

Perhaps one lasting result of the Depression and the small cheap cars it encouraged in such large numbers was the tremendous boost given to roadbuilding and improvement. Germany built many thousands of kilometres of *Autobahnen* with her vast army of unemployed; in Britain it was the era of the "by-pass". An increasing use of concrete in road-building enabled the process of construction to be speeded up when aided by more sophisticated machinery – itself the result of the development of the internal combustion engine, and everywhere the grey ribbons spread: Many are in use today still with their original surfaces.

With new arteries came roadside petrol stations in increasing numbers, cafés to cater for the needs of travellers and, inevitably, ribbon development of housing and industrial buildings. By 1939 Britain had caught up with her European neighbours, very few side roads being unsurfaced, and in America inter-city and inter-state travel was no longer the adventure it had been fifteen years before.

ABOVE: The Railton was made at the Cobham, Surrey, works which had formerly produced the Invicta. Designed by Reid Railton, it was an Anglo-American product based on a Terraplane or (later) a Hudson chassis, with Essex or Hudson engine and British coachwork. This is a 1935 Railton saloon.

LEFT: Derived from the Tipo B Grand Prix car, Alfa Romeo's 8C 2900B was a very high performance sports car with straight eight twin overhead camshaft engine and twin superchargers. Only 30 were made; some, like this coupé, with bodies by Pininfarina and Touring of Milan.

TOP: Originally an off-shoot of the German Daimler company, the Austro-Daimler factory became a separate entity in 1906. The ADR8, the firm's only eight cylinder car, of which this is a 1932 example, was introduced in 1930 and was phased out three years later.

59

Beetles & Minors

The second world war curbed motoring in all the combatant countries. In Britain there was an immediate anti-aircraft black-out and motorists driving at night had to mask their headlights to narrow slits. Petrol rationing was introduced after two weeks, and a month's civilian ration could easily be consumed in a day. In 1942, as U-boats took their toll of tankers, petrol for pleasure motoring was banned completely. Some motorists switched to gas, carried in roof-top containers, but these conversions were little more than curiosities.

Car factories were producing military vehicles, aircraft, engines of all kinds and such mundane but necessary items as steel helmets. In Britain, Austin made 120,000 military vehicles. Vauxhall built lorries and Churchill tanks. Daimler, though hit by 170 bombs, produced 6,500 scout cars and 2,500 armoured cars.

The biggest-selling vehicle of the Forties, and the most significant, was the quarter-ton American utility known as the Jeep (from the letters G.P. for general purpose). In 1940, Willys-Overland won a contract to produce 16,000; larger orders followed and Willys were joined in production by the mighty Ford company. By the end of the war 639,000 had been built.

The 3.352 m (11 ft) long Jeep had six forward and two reverse speeds, four-wheel drive, and it could go almost anywhere. The square "spamcans" were carried to war in gliders, were used as reconnaissance cars and gun carriers, and some were heavily armed for use by behind-the-lines forces. There was an amphibious version and another with flanged wheels to run on railway tracks, and even "double-decker" ambulances adapted for rail travel. The Jeep saw

service in every war theatre and continued to be produced after the war for private sale to farmers and others who wanted vehicles for cross-country work, a demand that led Rover to design the Land Rover in 1948.

Germany's equivalent of the Jeep was the *Kubelwagen*, or bucket car, based on pre-war designs by Ferdinand Porsche to meet Hitler's promise to provide a "people's car". It was 0.3 m longer than the Jeep, with an air-cooled, rear-mounted engine, first of 985 cc and later of 1,131 cc. Used extensively by the Afrika Korps, its versatility of application was similar to the Jeep's. Some 6,000 were built, and Porsche's experience with them was to have important repercussions after the war.

THE VOLKSWAGEN "BEETLE"

When the second world war ended in 1945 and pleasure motoring resumed, most of the new cars available were identical to models that had been on sale in 1939. However, the public bought them eagerly and there were long waiting lists. The buyer of a new British car could run it for several months to the envy of his neighbours and then sell it at a considerable profit. The more enterprising had their names on the waiting lists of several manufacturers at the same time, and eventually a covenant system was introduced under which a buyer had to undertake not to sell his new car for a specified period.

The first significant post-war car came from Germany and it was not in fact really new. It was the small car that Ferdinand Porsche had designed under the sponsorship of Hitler's "Strength through Joy" movement as a "people's car", first produced in 1938. It was this same car that provided the basis for the Kubelwagen – the Volkswagen "Beetle".

At the end of the war, the factory was in British hands and the first twelve thousand 1,131 cc Beetles produced during 1945 and 1946 were used by the British Army. The British could have retained control of the factory and the design, but they regarded the V.W. simply as an ugly little car and in 1949 relinquished the factory to the Germans, thereby passing up a world-beating export, the most successful car of the post-war period.

Although the Beetle was ugly, it was tremendously reliable and solidly built. Its doors closed with a satisfying clunk; the unburstable rear-mounted, air-cooled engine, uprated from 1,131 cc to 1,192 cc in 1954, and in the Sixties to 1.5 litres,

was to provide the basis for the high-performance Porsche. The styling scarcely changed over the years beyond an increase in the size of the rear window; the unchanging appearance was to become a boast of the V.W. advertising department.

The Beetle sold around the world. By 1961 the factory was producing a million a year and in 1972 it passed the 15 million sales of the Model T Ford nearly half a century earlier to become the world's best-selling car.

Meanwhile, the French were preparing to enter the world mass market. The Citroën 2CV was also based on a pre-war prototype that had been tested during the war. It was even uglier than the V.W., an incredibly stark and utilitarian vehicle with a nose-down attitude, a corrugated grey finish and a length of canvas as a roof, but the bonnet and wings were easily detachable for repairs. Its little 375 cc 9 bhp, twin-cylinder engine was capable of propelling it along roads or cart tracks. It was the kind of car which could be left out in the elements, with no

need to fuss over or polish it – and the French liked that. It sold 48,000 in 1950 and 78,000 in 1951. In 1955 the engine was uprated to 425 cc and by 1966 the 2CV had sold 2.5 million.

Italy's best-seller was also derived from a pre-war car, the Fiat 500. The post-war version, which became the Fiat 600 in 1955 when the 633 cc rear-mounted engine was uprated to 767 cc, was only 3 m (10 feet) long and 1.371 m (4 ft 6 in) wide, but by 1970 the midget had sold a million.

PREVIOUS PAGES: Brought over to Britain for evaluation after the war, an example of the Volkswagen "Beetle" was dismissed as "of no technical or practical merit". The evaluators would have been wiser if they had looked closely at the design career of its creator, Ferdinand Porsche, before giving it such a poor report. Working for both Austro-Daimler and Daimler (Mercedes), he had already been responsible for some extremely successful models. The Germans did not agree with the British assessment, and production of the VW Beetle eventually outstripped even Henry Ford's Model T. This is a 1953 model.

BRITISH BEST SELLER

Britain's first post-war best-seller, introduced in 1949, was more advanced because it stemmed from a completely new design by Alec Issigonis. The Morris Minor was small with a bulbous look, but it set new standards in road-holding for a popular car because of its torsion-bar independent front suspension and rack and pinion steering. It was a car utterly without vice, happily remembered by all who owned one.

The original 803 cc, side-valve engine was later uprated to 900, and then to 1,000 cc in ohv form following the merger with Austin, which gave it a top speed of about 116 km/h (72 mph) considered adequate at the time. By January 1961, a million Minors had been sold.

Other new models began to appear in Britain at the end of the Forties: the Standard Vanguard, an early example of what has come to be called a "fastback"; the Triumph range of distinctive razor-edged saloons, slightly reminiscent of pre-war Rolls-Royces; the Riley 1½ litre and 2½ litre sports saloons, considered by enthusiasts to be the last "proper Rileys" – in 1957 the firm lost its identity within the B.M.C. organization and the name continued merely as "badge engineering" on a rationalized model; and the MG TC, the first postwar car from Abingdon which was to become a plaything of rich Americans, particularly in Hollywood. In 1948, Vauxhall introduced Wyvern and Velox, which betrayed General Motors parentage by an abundance of chrome, and in 1951 Ford launched their Consul and Zephyr range.

Petrol rationing ended in Britain during 1950 (although it was to be reimposed in 1956 during the Suez crisis). An air ferry service from Lympne to Le Touquet had made transporting a car to the continent comparatively quick, and motoring abroad became more popular.

By the late 1950s the boom in private motoring was beginning to choke Britain's inadequate system of trunk routes, and in 1958 the M1 – the country's first motorway – from London to Birmingham was opened to traffic. The old horsepower tax, which made the road licence progressively more expensive according to engine capacity, was replaced in January 1948 by a flat rate, allowing designers to introduce more power to family saloons.

ABOVE: Known in prototype form as the "Mosquito", the Morris Minor designed by Alec Issigonis and marketed from 1949 was the first entirely new post-war Morris design. It remained in production until late 1970, and its rugged torsion bar independent front suspension survives in the Morris Marina.

LEFT: Developed initially as a three-wheeler by the American Bantam company, the Jeep had an inauspicious birth. In four-wheel form, however, and following development by Willys-Overland, it was built in vast numbers by both Willys and Ford during World War II. After the war it continued in production as a utility for use anywhere the going was rough.

RIGHT: Highlights of the Ford stand at the 1953 Motor Show in London were the new Anglia and Prefect models, both with side-valve 1172 cc power units. Steering, roadholding and performance were good for the day and both became best-sellers on the British market.

LESSONS FROM SPORT

Motor sport soon reawakened after the war. In Britain Brooklands remained in the hands of the aircraft industry, but a number of disused wartime airfields were available for use as racing circuits, and Silverstone, destined to become the greatest of them, opened for racing in 1948.

The first post-war racing cars, like production cars, were essentially pre-war models, and the Alfa-Romeo, with its supercharged 1.5 litre engine, reigned supreme until a new car and a new force entered motor racing under the prancing horse badge of Ferrari. Then Mercedes took over, followed by Britain with the Vanwall and the rear-engined Cooper.

Drivers' honours, once almost monopolized by the Latins, eventually yielded to the British. The Argentinian Juan-Manuel Fangio was the greatest for nearly a decade but finally gave way to Mike Hawthorn, in 1958 Britain's first world champion, and Stirling Moss, the greatest driver never to become world champion.

Superchargers had disappeared, new formulae reduced the size of engines, which were restricted in 1958 to pump petrol without alcohol additives, and the lessons learned in coaxing more power out of engines, which were first 2.5 litres and then shrank to 1.5 litres, were to play a major part in improving power units in production cars. This was the great justification for motor racing offered to those who felt it needed one: that developments pioneered at high speed on the Grand Prix circuits found their way eventually via high performance cars to the family saloon – and in the Fifties this was true.

The Fifties were a time of pioneering innovation, in racing, sports and road-going cars alike. The biggest change, perhaps, was the substitution of the unitary body for coachwork bolted on to a chassis. Tubeless tyres, though not a new idea, were reintroduced and established by Dunlop, while Michelin developed the radial-ply tyre (subject of much controversy before its eventual acceptance) to be used first, as usual, on high performance cars.

All-round independent suspension was first seen on a small family saloon in the 1959 Triumph Herald, which also had a collapsible steering wheel and a turning circle as tight as a London cab's.

Fuel-injection in place of a carburettor was introduced in 1952 by the six cylinder, 3 litre Mercedes-Benz 300 SL sports car, which won Le Mans that year, although it is best remembered for its gull-wing doors. The Citroën DS19 of 1955 used a unique self-levelling hydro-pneumatic suspension and had power-assisted braking and steering. For those who thought the system too complicated, the simpler ID19 version had the same advanced suspension without the power assistance. The little 590 cc, 92 km/h (57 mph) Dutch DAF, product of a firm noted for lorries, was a two-pedal (no gear-lever), belt-driven automatic.

Lightweight glass-fibre bodies came into use. America's Chevrolet Corvette six-cylinder sports car had one in 1953 while in England in 1957 the Lotus Elite was produced with a glass-fibre monocoque. A small but sweeping change, the use of the ignition key rather than a button for starting the engine, was pioneered by Chrysler in 1949.

Some of the innovations of the Fifties were well ahead of their time. In 1953, the first gas-turbine car was produced by Rover, drawing on wartime experience. In 1963, a 150 bhp Rover-B.R.M., driven by Graham Hill and Richie Ginther ran at Le Mans and averaged 174 km/h (108

Mercedes-Benz re-entered Grand Prix racing in 1954 backed by a 500-strong team of engineers and technical staff. The W196 seen here driven by Stirling Moss at Aintree housed a 2496 cc unit with fuel injection, desdromonic valve gear – and 190 bhp. It took Juan-Manuel Fangio to World Championship and Moss to the high-point of his career.

ABOVE: The Mini was introduced in 1959 and a new era of small saloon car racing flourished. Here Minis and Ford Anglias fight it out round Copse Corner at Silverstone.

RIGHT: Developed from the 220 Series saloon Mercedes-Benz cars the 300 SL sports model with "gull wing" doors took second and fourth places in the Mille Miglia in 1952 and first place at Le Mans. Many other successes followed during the car's six-year production life.

BELOW: Inheriting the power unit from the final development of the 1934 *"Traction Avant"*, the 1955 DS19 Citroën was as great a sensation when announced as its predecessor had been 21 years before.

mph), finishing an unofficial seventh.

Technical improvements were accompanied by styling changes. Roofs became lower, front wings were swept into the bonnet and rear wings into the boot. In 1957 there was a short-lived craze for high-swept rear fins. Headlamps became hooded, and in 1957 twin headlamps made their debut on Cadillac and Lincoln models. Split windscreens disappeared, replaced by wide, curved screens, and rear windows grew larger, while Daimler introduced electrically operated windows. Radiator grilles became more aggressive and cars became more colourful. Bizarre additions were the plastic insect-deflectors that appeared like a rash on bonnets around 1953, though they were inoffensive compared to the craze for dancing dolls behind windscreens.

There was a vogue for hard-tops on sports cars and for wood trimmings on estate wagons – but the strangest of all was for the bubble car in the mid-Fifties.

THE BUBBLE AND THE MINI

The bubble car was a tiny vehicle with two wheels at the front and usually one at the rear. Several British and Italian companies produced them – the Isetta, Meadows Frisky and also the German wartime aircraft manufacturers, Heinkel and Messerschmitt. Most housed single-cylinder engines and had their use as town conveyances but they were nearer to enclosed scooters than cars, and the bubble soon burst. Both Heinkel and Messerschmitt discontinued production in 1962, though for a time the Heinkel continued to be made in Britain under licence by Trojan.

Bigger three-wheelers also enjoyed some popularity in Britain among economy-minded motorists, but they were not cheap and most people wanted a "real" car, one with four wheels, some comfort and performance. There was the Ford Popular, introduced in 1954 with a 1,172 cc side-valve engine and three gears, and costing £391. It lacked glamour.

The answer was provided by Alec Issigonis, designer of the Morris Minor. His brilliant Mini was a product of the British Motor Corporation. Originally it was sold in two versions, the Austin Seven and the Mini-Minor, but the main difference was in the radiator grille, which fooled no one, and soon it became known just as the Mini.

This box-like car – a "brick", in the parlance of racing drivers who used it competitively, "with a wheel at each corner", gave ample room and marvellous roadholding. The original car had front-wheel drive, and an 848 cc four cylinder engine transverse-mounted to reduce the length of the bonnet and allow more interior space. Suspension was rubber in torsion. The finish was spartan, with sliding windows, outboard door hinges, and cable-operated interior door pulls. Gradually it became apparent that motorists were prepared to pay more for certain standards of comfort, and the fittings improved. Millionaires spent thousands on super-Minis with luxury finishes. The Mini became a classless car.

Inevitably, too, in view of its roadholding, sporting versions were developed, including the Mini-Cooper of 1962. Soon there were classes for it in motor sport, and in 1964 Paddy Hopkirk and Henry Liddon drove a Mini-Cooper to victory in the Monte Carlo Rally – the first of a hat-trick of victories in the event. The Mini sold in millions from its first introduction and continues to do so.

NEW NAMES AND OLD

New names rose to prominence in the Forties and Fifties, perhaps the most distinguished of which was the Swedish firm of Saab. Other countries, including Poland, Turkey, Spain and Russia, produced their first private cars for sale to the public. At the same time, familiar names disappeared in liquidations and in mergers. Armstrong-Siddeley, Lea-Francis, Allard, Frazer-Nash, H.R.G. and Invicta were among the discontinued. It was the age of super-mass-production with little room for the small company.

Not all the big companies were successful. The classic cautionary tale of the motor industry remains that of Ford's Edsel model which, despite all Ford's

ABOVE: Offered by BMC as either an Austin Seven or a Morris Mini-Minor, the first versions had an 848 cc four cylinder engine in the now-familiar transverse location, front-wheel drive and rubber suspension.

BELOW LEFT: The 1956 Suez crisis with its resultant petrol rationing encouraged the production of some strange little machines designed for economy. This Meadows Frisky, introduced in 1957, was a typical example though rather longer-lived than most.

resources and know-how in marketing, lost the firm 250 million dollars between 1958 and 1960. It was a spectacular failure, made for a gap in the motor market that did not, in fact, exist.

Finally, there was a nostalgia boom for old cars. The Veteran Car Club had been formed as far back as 1930 and the film *Genevieve*, made in 1952, created an interest in old cars which today is greater than ever among those who had never owned a veteran.

At Beaulieu in Hampshire, Lord Montagu founded (originally with three cars) the Montagu Motor Museum – now the National Motor Museum – in memory of his father, a distinguished pioneer motorist. In 1960 came the first public auction of old cars, which now sell in the same way as rare paintings and objets d'art at Sotheby's and Christie's.

To describe the modern car as "fool-proof" might be an exaggeration, but it was true that as well as bringing technical improvements the Forties and Fifties also brought an acceptance of the concept of built-in obsolescence. Cars were no longer being built for longevity. They had become possessions to be changed and traded in at intervals.

RIGHT: Ten years of experiment produced the Citroën 2CV in 1949. Designer Boulanger's 375 cc model was a new concept, pared down to the utility demands of the stark post-war era. This modern version shows that the car has changed little in appearance over the past 29 years.

BELOW: Regarded as one of the first genuine sports cars produced in post-war America the Ford Thunderbird was introduced in 1955. The two-seater housed a 5.1 litre engine of 225 bhp and had a top speed of 182 km/h (113 mph). This is a 1957 model.

The 60's and 70's

General affluence kept motoring booming in the sixties. By 1963, the British licensing authorities, running out of numbers for registration plates, introduced suffix letters. By the time of the 1971 census, more than half of the households in England and Wales had at least one car, and one in ten had two cars or more.

Roads, particularly motorways, were at last increasing, although the United Kingdom still had only a third of the motorway mileage of Germany. The demand for fuel at all hours, coupled with increasing wages, led to the introduction in 1961 of self-service petrol pumps. The car became virtually a mobile drawing room with comfortable seats and music on cartridges and cassettes. Tape-playing units were allied to V.H.F. radios and stereo speakers soon became commonplace.

Traffic congestion worsened during the early sixties and the authorities reacted with complex, one-way traffic systems, millions of gallons of yellow paint along kerbs, more legislation and more law enforcement. The Ministry of Transport vehicle test was introduced in 1960 and, though far from stringent, succeeded in clearing some of the most dangerous old cars from the road, although the manner of its operation – by the garage industry – was much criticized. The police introduced radar speed traps in 1959 and the breathalyser in 1967. Compulsory fitting of seat belts also came in 1967, together with an overall speed limit of 113 km/h (70 mph) even on motorways.

But in 1964, a 35-mile traffic jam outside Torquay gave warning of horrors to come, and in the same year there was an even more ominous occurrence – a 100-car pile-up on the M1. "Motorway madness" became a familiar newspaper headline, particularly when there was fog.

PREVIOUS PAGES Scotsman Jackie Stewart first won the World Championship in 1969 driving a Matra, and followed this up in 1971 with another win at the wheel of a Tyrrell.

TOP: When Ford of Great Britain first offered the Cortina in 1963 some considered it old-fashioned, with its rear wheel drive, its 1.2 and 1.5 litre engine form, and its conventional suspension. Ford proved them wrong very quickly and the Cortina became the top-selling British-made car.

ABOVE: First seen in 1970, the Range Rover is one of the most popular go-anywhere vehicles ever produced. Powered by the 3½ litre V8 Rover unit through a four-speed gearbox (high and low ratio) and three differentials to all four wheels, this smart yet rugged car can reach 158 km/h (98 mph).

CHANGING SHAPE OF CARS

Meanwhile, the nature of cars was changing. The success of the Mini led to more front-wheel drive cars. In this the Mini had not been first: Citroën had used front-wheel drive since the Thirties and Saab since 1950. Peugeot, Renault, Lancia, Audi, Simca and N.S.U. followed. In 1963, B.M.C. introduced the Austin 1100 front-wheel drive range with Hydrolastic suspension, which, from 1965 was also built into the Minis. In 1971, the Citroën GS, a sophisticated, four-cylinder 1,015-cc front-wheel-drive car capable of 146 km/h (91 mph), was to be voted "Car of the Year" in many polls.

The rear-engine revolution initiated by Volkswagen lost some impetus, al-though V.W. themselves remained true to the design. The 875 cc overhead camshaft Hillman Imp, the Rootes Group's answer to the Mini launched in 1963, was virtually the last new car with a rear engine, and it never sold as well as the Mini.

Many manufacturers, for example Ford and Vauxhall, remained faithful to the conventional front-engine, rear-wheel drive formula. Ford introduced the medium-size Cortina in 1963 and in 1968 the smaller Escort, a two-door saloon replacing the Anglia, which had sold well over a million in eight years. In 1964 Vauxhall started producing the 1,057 cc Viva, almost identical to the German Opel Kadett, at £566.

More expensive and sophisticated pro-

ducts included Jaguar's sporty E-type giving 265 bhp and 241 km/h (150 mph) from a six cylinder, 3.8 litre engine; it had disc brakes on all four instead of just the front wheels. The more stately Jaguar XJ6 (1968) came with a six cylinder, 2.8 or 4.2 litre engine.

The Jensen FF (£5,340), with a 6.3 litre engine, was the first to boast Ferguson four-wheel drive and Dunlop anti-skid braking. Triumph's 2.5 PI (1968) was the first British saloon to be equipped with fuel injection as a standard feature.

In the realm of the exotic sports car, Lotus led in 1966 with its Europa, powered by a 1.5 litre Renault engine, and with a glass-fibre body so streamlined and low one could practically trip over it.

The 1971 Range Rover, with a 3.5 litre V8 engine, combined the ruggedness of a Land Rover with the comfort and near-100 mph performance of a Rover saloon.

There was no shortage of innovatory design in the Sixties. The 1963 Lotus Elan had retractable headlamps; the 1968 Citroën DS revived swivelling head-lamps that turned with the road wheels. The Wankel rotary engine was a revolutionary concept, introduced first in the N.S.U. Spider with a capacity equal to about 500 cc and then used with the equivalent of a 2 litre capacity in the 1968 N.S.U. R080, a front-wheel drive, semi-automatic. The Wankel, it must be said, was beset by failure in its early stages.

ABOVE: Mass-production – but the individual car worker still has an important part to play on the mechanized assembly line. Here at Leyland the transformation from body shell to motor car begins, and by the end of the day both cars will probably be on their way by transporter to the dealer network.

CENTRE: Volkswagen earned a reputation for establishing a "permanent" body style, while constantly improving the mechanical elements. While the Beetle is the best-known example of this principle, the Kombi has now been in production for well over twenty years and still looks thoroughly modern. Incorporating the same air-cooled rear-mounted engine upon which VW's fortunes have been based, it is a full twelve-seater, and is also available as a mobile caravan conversion.

In motor sport, too, cars changed – not only in visible ways, exemplified by the wings that began to sprout in 1968. The biggest influence came from the Ford organization, which set out to change its image from makers of cheap, mass-produced cars by pouring money into prototype sports car racing. It spent a small fortune before achieving its object of breaking Ferrari domination in this class in 1966, when a 7 litre Ford, driven by Bruce McLaren and Chris Amon, won Le Mans. Ford won again for the next three years.

In Grand Prix racing, Ford backed the small Cosworth factory which produced a 3 litre, V8 engine of 400 bhp to succeed the 1.5 litre Coventry-Climax unit, which incidentally was originally designed for fire pumps. The Cosworth unit powered the majority of Formula One cars, bringing victory, among others, to Graham Hill and Lotus and Jackie Stewart and Tyrrell.

At a lower level, the 105E Anglia engine dominated Formula Junior events. Ford also introduced their own Formula Ford category for cars using Cortina 1.6 litre engines. The cost of motor racing was becoming exorbitant, and although cars began to look like advertising hoardings, money was always in short supply. Impoverished enthusiasts turned to saloon car racing.

RIGHT: Drag racing started in the USA in 1950 as a way of encouraging young men to race their cars off public roads. Basically a straight quarter-mile sprint with only two cars competing at a time, it has now become extremely sophisticated, with runs timed at less than 5 seconds, and terminal speeds of over 480 km/h (300 mph). The sport has also developed into a "workshops contest" where the engineer with the best engine/chassis ideas is as important as the driver. It is also the motor sport with the least fatalities.

LEFT: Sponsored by the Marlboro cigarette company, the Marlboro-BRM P 180 of 1972 was designed as a semi-monocoque with twin rear radiators and a tubular rear subframe supporting the 3 litre V12 BRM engine. Driven here by jockey's son Peter Gethin (who had won the Italian Grand Prix the previous year by 24 inches!) the car developed 440 bhp at 10,750 rpm.

CENTRE: The Mk 25 Lotus heralded a completely new technique in building Formula One racing car bodies in 1962. A monocoque riveted box construction conceived by Colin Chapman, it was more rigid than conventional tubular space frames. The following year, with the Coventry-Climax V8 installed, Jim Clark gained seven wins in *grandes epreuves*, including five in Formula 1 races, and became World Champion.

BELOW: In 1967, the year he won the World Championship, Denny Hulme left Jack Brabham to join fellow New Zealander Bruce McLaren as a driver in the Cam-Am races. The arrangement proved successful, three races being won out of six in the first season, and Hulme won the Cam-Am Championship in 1968. Here he drives a Formula 1 McLaren.

ABOVE: Faithful to its original concept the Corvette, often called America's only sports car (except by those whose loyalty to Ford demands that recognition for the early Thunderbird) has, since its debut in 1953, kept its sporting lines and performance. Its body is still fibreglass and its centre of gravity probably the lowest of any American production car. Passing through some 50 different forms in its life the spectacular Corvette has emerged a stable, fast-moving thoroughbred.

ABOVE: Chrysler started production of the famous "letter" range in 1955 with the 300, using mainly their 6½ litre V8 engine. This is the 1960 300F, with an aggressive 375 bhp under the hood and a long list of NASCAR (National Association for Stock Car Auto Racing) speed records to its credit.

PREVIOUS PAGES: The most popular "platform" on which to build a "customised" car from the wheels up is the immortal Ford Model T, which often sports a V8 powerpack, supercharged and unsilenced, with metal flake paintwork and lashings of chrome – just in case the spectator fails to notice it . . .

CRUSADES

An anti-car movement developed in America and spread across the Atlantic. It began with Ralph Nader and his henchmen, known as "Nader's Raiders", who launched an onslaught on safety standards with the slogan "Unsafe at any speed". They caught public imagination by pointing out that the car was responsible for 130,000 fatalities and 1.7 million serious casualties in the western world *every year*.

Seat belts had almost become accepted equipment, but they were not enough for the crusaders. Experiments began into the use of air bags, which inflated in the event of a crash to place a cushioning bumper between front seat passengers and the windscreen, dashboard and controls.

The safety crusade was followed by a drive against pollution. This began in Los Angeles, where the sky is notoriously obscured by smog, chiefly because of curious atmospheric conditions, but certainly not helped by fumes from the city's cars. California introduced legislation to eliminate toxic elements in car exhaust fumes and this lead was taken up throughout America. It was calculated that 105 million vehicles burned 200 million gallons of petrol every day.

In his State of the Union message in January 1970, the American President declared: "The automobile is our worst polluter of air. Adequate control requires further advances in engine design and fuel composition. We shall intensify our research, set increasingly strict standards and strengthen enforcement procedures – and we shall do it now." By the end of the year, the Senate had made anti-pollution legislation law with a programme of increasingly stringent controls to last until 1980.

Firms spent millions on reducing exhaust-fume poisons and on research into alternative means of power such as steam and electricity, but the anti-motoring lobby grew stronger. In Britain its grievances were the architectural horror of Birmingham's Spaghetti Junction, too many new motorways and too few traffic-free precincts.

IMPORTS AND MERGERS

Meanwhile, the Japanese, who had already revolutionized the world's camera and motor cycle industries, turned their attention to the motor car. At first, in the Sixties, they made conventional, front-engine, rear-wheel-drive models, but soon rapidly expanded into all varieties of layout. Mazda took out a licence to build the Wankel rotary engine and became the first firm to put it into mass production. In 1976, the Japanese staged their first Grand Prix race on a new circuit at the foot of Mount Fuji.

Japanese marketing of cars adversely affected both American and British manufacturers; the situation was aggravated by an aggressive sales launch from manufacturers in the Communist countries of Eastern Europe, who competed with extremely cheap cars like Czechoslovakia's Skoda, Russia's Lada and Poland's Fiat 125P.

In Britain, imported cars were a mere eight per cent of total sales at the start of the Sixties. Ownership of a foreign car was a sign of individuality, or even

RIGHT: The Sixties saw the beginning of a European marketing campaign from Japan. This 180B Datsun Bluebird displays compact Western lines, and with an overhead camshaft, 1770 cc engine, has a top speed of 166 km/h (103 mph).

BELOW: Volkswagen Beetle 1977. Hardly changed in outward appearance from the 1953 version on page 60–61, the Beetle soldiers on in many parts of the world, although developing countries are its main sales markets today.

eccentricity, but by the mid-Seventies imports rose to around 40 per cent, and home manufacturers started to accuse their foreign counterparts of "dumping" cars at artificially low prices.

The buyer seemed happy. Surveys showed that he felt foreign cars to be better finished and more reliable than British. One carried out by the Consumers' Association and published in *Motoring Which* in 1976 showed that for reliability their members favoured Datsun, Renault, Toyota, Volvo, V.W.-Audi and Mazda, in that order.

Old-established car firms, beset by labour problems and difficulty in meeting delivery dates, were having serious problems. In the first half of 1970 the Rootes Group lost £7.5 million and Vauxhall lost £2 million, while production in America fell to its lowest for nine years.

Mergers became more frequent. Chrysler, which had gained control of the Rootes Group in 1964, renamed it Chrysler (U.K.) in 1970 and added Simca and Matra to its Hillman, Singer and Sunbeam models, soon replacing those names with that of Chrysler.

Fiat acquired Lancia, Ferrari and Abarth. V.W. bought N.S.U. and Audi. But the biggest merger of all was the one which in 1967 created British Leyland from the Leyland group, which had taken over Jaguar, which had taken over Daimler. It brought together virtually all the remaining British owned motor firms in one giant corporation, responsible for such different makes as Austin, Daimler, Jaguar, M.G., Morris, Riley, Rover, Triumph, Vanden Plas and Wolseley. The accumulation of so many factories with different outlooks and conditions of work took years to digest.

Meanwhile, Ford was rationalizing its European models so that British and German Fords became more standardized.

In 1976 Britain's ten best-selling cars were:

1. Ford Cortina
2. Ford Escort
3. Leyland Mini
4. Leyland Marina
5. Leyland Allegro
6. Vauxhall Viva/Magnum
7. Chrysler Avenger
8. Chrysler Hunter
9. Leyland Princess
10. Datsun Sunny

THE OIL CRISIS

1973 was a nightmare year for motorists and the motor industry. Costs had been rising steadily, but now they exploded, touched off by the Arab–Israeli conflict in October – the Yom Kippur War. A petrol drought followed, long queues formed outside filling stations and ration coupons were distributed (but never actually used) in Britain.

As a result, speed limits were introduced for fuel economy, 80 km/h (50 mph) being the maximum permitted on single carriageways. On the continent there were no-motoring days. Then it became apparent that there was no actual shortage of petrol but that the Arab producers were going to demand a much higher price for crude oil. They had noted the tax added to petrol prices in western countries and reasoned that, if the motorist could afford them, he could afford to pay more for the fuel itself. In 15 months, the price of petrol doubled; pumps were breaking down because their gauges overheated.

PREVIOUS PAGES: Datsun's 260Z, developed from the slightly smaller version of this Japanese company's sports offering, houses a potent six cylinder seven-bearing 2.6 litre unit which runs on low-lead fuel.

INSERT TOP LEFT: Mazda's top model range includes this 929 saloon and coupé with 1,796 cc engine of conventional design.

INSERT BOTTOM LEFT: A 1977 addition to Honda offerings was the Accord, launched in Japan and the USA in 1976. A 1,599 cc engine transversely mounted drives the front wheels, developing 80 bhp.

INSERT BOTTOM RIGHT: Some Japanese cars look more sporting than they are, but this stylish Toyota Celica ST Liftback has an 82 bhp 1,968 cc single overhead camshaft unit and top speed of over 160 km/h (100 mph).

Naturally, petrol sales fell and average annual mileage declined. In the Thirties, the Automobile Association had calculated that the average yearly mileage was 12,000 miles. Since 1947 it had worked out at 10,000 miles a year. In 1976 the average dropped to 8,000 miles a year. It was reckoned that the average motorist was spending £10 a week to keep his car on the road – and that excluded depreciation. For many, the cost was greater than that of the mortgage repayments on their houses.

Licence fees rose sharply, and so did garage charges. Motorists began to omit services. New car registrations declined, falling from a record 1.6 million in 1973 to 1.3 million in 1974 and 1.2 million in 1975. In the factories, car workers were

ABOVE: The French build their cars ruggedly – sometimes to the detriment of quiet and comfort, but this Peugeot 504 (the model was first seen in 1968) combines luxury with the lusty qualities needed to win international rallies. The East African Safari Rally is a Peugeot favourite and here British drivers Shankland and Barton plough their way through some typical African country in the 1975 event.

FAR LEFT: The Jaguar XJ series captured a wide market in the 1970's with its sleek and handsome appearance and its rapid but safe speed, especially in V12 specification. Voted Car of the Year by the Press in 1969 the XJ6 sold so successfully that there has always been a waiting list for these cars from the Leyland company.

laid off and put on short time, and British Leyland and Chrysler U.K. needed vast sums of money from the British Government to avoid more redundancies in a country where unemployment figures were already alarming.

At the time of the 1974 Motor Show, even a Mini cost more than £1,000, compared with £470 in 1965. There was only one British car on offer at less than £1,000 – the Hillman Imp (£998) – but that was for the basic model with no heater.

The price of a Mini was in fact £1,027. Yet the engine cost less than £50 to build and the body shell about £100. Where did the rest go? This was the company's breakdown of costs.

Tax and V.A.T.: £180
Labour: £150

Materials, including steel, rubber and plastic: £324
Advertising and promotion: £3
Company profit, dividends, interest on borrowed money and plant investment: £105
Dealer's profit at 17.5 per cent: £175
Losses from strikes: £90.

Only about 46 per cent of the price was represented by materials and work on the car. In the case of a Rolls-Royce, the company was turning out a Camargue every week at a price of more than £31,000, taxation representing nearly £5,000.

Economists tried to lighten the gloom by calculating that cars were still cheap in real terms, by which they meant the proportion of income needed to buy and run one. For example, the cost of a Mini

ABOVE: Lancia, part of the Fiat complex since 1969, first offered the Stratos in production form in 1973. With its Ferrari Dino V6 engine at the rear, this short-tailed low-profile sporting vehicle has now scored a string of major rally successes.

in 1976 represented only 28 per cent of the average gross wage, compared to 50 per cent in 1960 and 70 per cent before the second world war. In the Thirties, they pointed out, it cost over £90 to run a small car and the average manual worker earned only £127 a year.

However, the average manual worker, who had grown accustomed to the convenience of a car, found this small consolation when he could no longer meet the difference between the trade-in price on his old model and the cost of a new one.

1977
and the future

In 1976 the world's most expensive car was ordered from the Surrey firm of Panther West Winds by an undisclosed buyer, thought to be either an Arab Sheikh or a South American head of state. The interior was to be circular, air-conditioned, lined with mink and suede and incorporate a cocktail bar, refrigerator, television and hi-fi. The exterior was to be armour-plated, bullet- and mine-resistant, and with a roof mounting for a machine-gun. The cost: more than £60,000.

This vehicle was, of course, unique, but luxury cars are still being made and offered for sale, even if the oil princes are the only people who can afford them. General economy, however, has dictated a mass market trend towards small, efficient cars rather than uninspired, big cars.

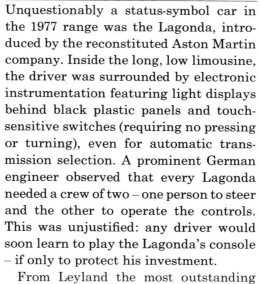

Unquestionably a status-symbol car in the 1977 range was the Lagonda, introduced by the reconstituted Aston Martin company. Inside the long, low limousine, the driver was surrounded by electronic instrumentation featuring light displays behind black plastic panels and touch-sensitive switches (requiring no pressing or turning), even for automatic transmission selection. A prominent German engineer observed that every Lagonda needed a crew of two – one person to steer and the other to operate the controls. This was unjustified: any driver would soon learn to play the Lagonda's console – if only to protect his investment.

From Leyland the most outstanding car for some years was the Rover 3500, a five-door design with exceptional interior space and excellent, all-round visibility. The 3.5 litre V8 engine had been up-rated to give 155 bhp, controlled through an exceptionally good new five-speed gearbox. Standard equipment was unusually comprehensive and the car won top marks from experts for its performance, economy, handling, transmission, instruments, heating and ventilation.

Inevitably, the most talked-about car in Britain during the late seventies was the Ford Fiesta (with ten different choices of specification), for this was the company's answer to the Mini. It cost more, but it offered more room, a better driving position and better visibility than the Mini, and it bore a remarkable resemblance to its newer small-car rivals, especially the V.W. Polo.

Ford's most important evolutionary change was in the successful Cortina series, the fourth such major change. The Cortina acquired the body of its sister car, the German Ford Taunus, and was made available in 17 different versions, from a 1.3 litre economy car to the luxurious 2 litre Ghia.

In the 924, Porsche produced their first front-engined car with rear-wheel drive. The engine was water-cooled and the gearbox was at the back, and it seemed that its only main Porsche feature was the wide use of V.W. components. Volkswagen themselves brought out the Golf GTI with a 110 bhp version of the 1,588 cc ohc engine and Bosch K Jetronic fuel injection: this proved to be an outstanding sports saloon with handling and comfort to match.

The 1977 Mercedes-Benz 200 to 280E range became available in the U.K. and there were seven models in the small W123 class range. The leader, the 280E, looked almost identical to the larger "S" class models.

France entered the lists with new or modified models from Citroën, Peugeot and Renault. Citroën's LN was a new Mini. Peugeot made major modifications to their small 104, giving it a fifth door. Renault's adaptations were designed to make up for omissions in their range. All versions of the 15 acquired the 1,289 cc engine, making them capable of 145 km/h (90 mph), while the leader in the middle range was the 14 with an enlarged Peugeot engine of 1,218 cc set transversely and inclined at 72 degrees. It was a shorter car than the Renault 12 or 16 but the five-door body provided nearly as much space.

In Sweden, Saab introduced the 99GLE, a luxury, automatic executive car, and gave the 99EMS a sportier suspension,

PREVIOUS PAGES: The Ford Fiesta-based Corrida has double-hinged gull-wings and a drop-down boot extension – very much a car for the future with its low line and cubist appearance. Power comes from the Ford 1117 cc unit.

ABOVE LEFT: Still a car for the future although it was first designed and built as an experimental vehicle in 1969, the gull-winged Mercedes-Benz C111 Wankel-engined coupé illustrates what tomorrow's car may look like. The original housed a three rotor unit, but in 1970 a 350 bhp four rotor engine was fitted, giving a top speed of 306 km/h (190 mph). Germany's Daimler-Benz company decided that the market was not ready for this exhilarating car. . .

FAR LEFT: First seen in Britain in October 1977 this Renault 20TL (overtaking, left of picture) was the French motor manufacturer's latest offering in the just-over 1½ litre market.

CENTRE LEFT: The 1977 Lagonda from the Aston Martin stable combines an aerodynamic and highly futuristic body designed by William Towns with the well-proved V8 Aston Martin engine. A sensation when announced at the 1976 Motor Show, the car bristled with new ideas, including electronic instrumentation with its own mini-computer.

NEAR LEFT: Porsche produced a front-engined car – the 924 – for the first time in 1977. Rear-wheel drive was the only gesture to convention, however, and the expected highest-quality engineering can be seen under the cladding.

ABOVE: Britain's Triumph TR7, with the 105 hp version of the 2 litre engine. Designed primarily for export to the USA the two-seater sports car from Leyland has a maximum speed of around 180 km/h (110 mph).

RIGHT: Newcomer in 1972, the Audi 80, a smaller version of the 100, was restyled in 1976. In 1300 or 1500 cc form the engine is a single overhead camshaft unit with power up to 85 bhp. Front wheel drive gives this car good road holding in winter weather, and low fuel consumption appeals to buyers in an oil-short world.

suggesting a more powerful engine to follow; they also turned the Combi coupé into a five-door model. The Volvo 343 was a Swedish–Dutch–French hybrid with a strong Volvo body, Daf variomatic transmission and a 1.4 litre version of the Renault 12 engine. The three-door hatchback included a prominent lip at the rear to act as a spoiler.

Meanwhile, in Japan, Mazda introduced a twin-rotary engine said to be longer-lasting than previous versions and extremely smooth, though the ride and handling of the car itself still came in for criticism. In 1977, the Wankel remained the most exciting engine since Gottlieb Daimler's, but times were against it, for

it was handicapped by a thirst for fuel. The cost of petrol was over-riding all other considerations in motoring, but did bring compensations including greater engine efficiency regardless of size (a worthwhile development by any standard) and greater competition and sophistication in small-car design.

At the same time, big manufacturers' concern over industrial unrest and rising production costs encouraged them to make models only in one country for multinational design, or to produce engines in one country and marry them to bodies and other components built in another. Innovations such as the fifth door and run-flat-for-100-miles safety

tyres also persisted in new designs.

More high-performance cars, like the B.M.W. 633 coupé and the V.W. Golf GTI, acquired fuel injection, and more models offered economical diesel-engined versions, among them Citroën and V.W. Sports cars such as the Lancia Beta Monte Carlo continued to adopt the mid-engine position. On many cars, steering wheels lost most of their spokes and some became elliptical rather than circular. Road wheels were "styled" with perforated discs, and head restraints increased the height of front seats. In two instances, cars with gull-wing doors – used on the 300 SL Mercedes of the mid-Fifties – were seen once again, on the Mercedes-

Benz C111 *Versuchswagen* (research and development car), and on the Ford Corrida, a good, scaled-down imitation of the German product, based on the recent Fiesta.

In general, styling was simpler and more functional. Gone were excesses such as heavily chromed radiator grilles. Cars were safer and faster. Before the war, few family cars had been capable of exceeding 96 km/h (60 mph); in 1977 they could manage a steady 145 km/h (90 mph) – where permitted. Intervals between servicing (which had once involved a weekly session of oiling) grew longer, although this was largely prompted by increased garage costs.

CAUSE FOR CONCERN

General improvement has, until recently, failed to touch one of the modern motor car's greatest drawback's – rust. Unitary construction, which reduced manufacturing costs and allowed greatly increased production, brought with it the use of thinner pressed steel, and this can result in some cars being literally eaten away by rust after 15 years.

As consumerism has grown, written coverage of motoring and motor products has become more honest and inquiring, and the car buyer more aware of his rights in law as to what he may expect from maker and dealer.

For the motorist's holiday, package tours have been developed which provide him with a route and ready-booked hotels along it. Continental travel has been made more available by the possibility of buying or hiring caravans or motor caravans, or even trailer-borne tents. Cars may be readily hired almost anywhere.

Indeed, only on the continent can the British motorist still find miles of road with scarcely a car in sight. Yet even there overall speed limits are proliferating, parking restrictions becoming tighter, and petrol even more expensive than in Great Britain. To be a motorist anywhere requires patience, tolerance, and a fat wallet.

END OF AN ERA

That remains the situation. The car, which began life as a rich man's plaything and became a servant of the people, is now fighting for survival – and not just because of doubts about petrol supplies. That is not so alarmist as it seems. With 220 million vehicles on the roads of the world it is the petrol-engined car's very numbers which make its future a matter for conjecture.

The car brought a new freedom, which is now endangered. Cars do cause noise, pollution, congestion and deaths. The threshold of tolerance is approaching, and for some has already been reached – for example, those with the misfortune to live under or near a busy flyover.

There have been some farsighted developments. The scaling-down of engine capacities, the introduction of fifth gears, the reintroduction of overdrive and the use of radial steel-ply tyres with less rolling resistance have all helped cut fuel consumption. Seat belts and head restraints, rigid shells, collapsible steering wheels, padded fascias and the invention

BELOW LEFT: The Renault 5 is typical of the front-wheel-drive hatchbacks that now dominate Europe's small-car market. Options include engines of 782 cc, 956 cc, and 1289 cc, the last (in the 5TS) giving a top speed of well over 90 mph.

BELOW: The Peugeot 104 competes directly with the Renault 5, also offering three engine sizes. Top of the range is this 104 ZS, with a performance similar to that of the 5TS. Note the head restraints, now a common option even in small cars.

ABOVE: Market rival to the Ford Fiesta is the Volkswagen Polo, the company's smallest car, with practical three-door layout. It has a 1093 cc unit, a short-stroke version of the slightly larger and very similar VW Golf.

RIGHT: The most talked-about car in Britain in 1977 – the Ford Fiesta. Looking very like similar products from Germany and France, the new contender for the very-small-car market houses a 957 cc or 1117 cc high compression transverse engine driving the front wheels.

of self-sealing, re-inflating tyres have improved safety. New regulations, pioneered in the United States, have reduced the emission of toxic fumes. But it is impossible to abolish them completely, or to silence noise, or do away with congestion, or to ban accidents.

For its part, the motor industry has spent heavily in recent years on research into ways of reducing pollution. All forms of combustion produce undesirable by-products such as carbon monoxide, unburnt hydrocarbons and soot, but there are systems more efficient than the petrol engine as it exists. Diesel fuel, for example, produces only a thirtieth of the toxic fumes of petrol. Diesels have become more popular, although generally they lack the flexible response of the petrol engine. There has been research into the catalytic converter, which saves fuel and gives quieter running on unleaded petrol, and into the stratified charge system. This latter involves modifying the engine to make the petrol-air mixture richer near the plug but weaker elsewhere. Ignition takes place readily, and the

leaner mixture burns more completely, giving greater economy and low emission of fumes.

The gas turbine, quiet, powerful and running on low-grade leaded fuel, but complex and costly to make, is yet another option; so is the Stirling engine, using external combustion, first devised by a Scot during the 19th century.

With petrol engine improvement there has also been research into other forms of power. Steam is quieter and less of a pollutant than the petrol engine, but poses problems of weight and responsiveness to the controls. Electricity, ultimate in the sense that it is completely silent and clean, has the drawback of requiring a frequent recharge for the heavy batteries.

Some 250 experimental electric town cars have been produced, but they normally present only two, unsatisfactory alternatives: either reasonable mileage between charges and a low speed, or reasonable speed and an absurdly small mileage. A General Motors prototype, for example, had a range of 93 km at

40 km/h (58 miles at 25 mph) or 75.5 km at 48 km/h (47 miles at 30 mph).

Some believe that the future lies with a hybrid, involving an electric motor for town use and a small internal combustion engine for main roads which would power a generator to recharge the batteries.

However the situation is eventually resolved, it is certain that the internal combustion engine will be with us for some decades – until there is a fundamental reappraisal of all road transport, its appearance and function. This needs to be part of a larger reappraisal of all forms of transport. Governments have been urging greater use of public transport to relieve road congestion, and high-speed trains, even monorails, are becoming a reality; but so far no government has planned an integrated transport policy, setting out the projected roles of railways, waterways and road transport.

Until this is done, a question mark will hang over the motor car, the invention that has, directly or indirectly, changed the way of life of millions during this century more than anything else.

The Great Marques

In the years which have passed since the internal combustion engine first coughed into life, there have been well over 5,000 hopeful attempts at motor car manufacture, of which only a handful were successful. Some expired quietly without a single car being completed, some are still with us, excellent, reliable mass products, and a few have earned reputations that set them apart from their competitors. These are the great names of the motoring age, synonymous with quality, elegance, speed or sheer luxury – for those who can afford it.

THE BEST CAR IN THE WORLD

"The quality will remain after the price is forgotten." Although it was not Rolls-Royce themselves who first coined the best-car slogan, it was largely as a result of the philosophy of Frederick Henry Royce, quoted above, that the press were so complimentary about his cars.

The son of a Lincolnshire flour miller, Henry Royce's early career indicated little of what was to come. His first job, as a newspaper boy for W. H. Smith & Son at Clapham, was uneventful; later he was apprenticed to the Great Northern Railway, and by 1883, in his twentieth year, he had formed his own tiny company in a small workshop in Cooke Street, Manchester, making lamp holders and

electric bells. From such beginnings, Royce progressed to dynamos and electric cranes, and in 1903 began tinkering with a second-hand, two cylinder Decauville light car. He built a 10 hp car of his own design, a considerable improvement on the Decauville, but incorporated a number of the French car's features of which he approved. On 1 April 1904, the car was ready and, to traditional tin-banging applause, and a few pointed remarks about the date, the first Royce was driven out on a test run.

It proved quiet, reliable and altogether better than its two cylinder contemporaries, and soon caught the attention of young Welsh aristocrat, the Hon. Charles Stewart Rolls, third son of Lord Llangattock. Rolls at this time was selling Panhards, Minervas and Mors from premises in Brook Street, Mayfair, and so impressed was he with the Royce that, after some argument, an agreement was drawn up by which total production from the Royce works would be sold by C. S. Rolls & Co. under the name of Rolls-Royce. The company of Rolls-Royce Limited was formed in 1906.

"I am rarely tempted into the realms of prophecy, but I venture to say Messrs Rolls and Co will make a high reputation for themselves through their all-British made cars." Motor News, December 1904.

Four and six cylinder cars followed, and in 1906 a Rolls-Royce four cylinder Twenty won the second Isle of Man Tourist Trophy. At a time when the petrol engine was often unresponsive, and always erratic and noisy, the Rolls-Royce on its first tests proved quite the opposite; Henry Swindley (owner of *The Autocar* magazine) was moved to say "With the pedal alone one can almost make the car play cat's cradle".

However, it was the Silver Ghost, its name taken from the silvery aluminium finish of its bodywork and the remarkable silence of its six cylinder engine, which established the lofty reputation of the company, successfully completing a 24,140 km (15,000 mile) R.A.C.-observed trial in 1907. In 1911, a car was driven from London to Edinburgh and back entirely in top gear. With only minor improvements the Silver Ghost remained the sole Rolls-Royce product until 1922, when a smaller Twenty was introduced, and continued in production until 1925. Its successor, the Phantom I, was replaced in 1930 by the Phantom II, and by this time the Rolls-Royce was accepted as the standard for the world.

Charles Rolls did not long enjoy his fame. He was killed while landing his Wright biplane on 11 July 1920. Henry Royce's health was failing, the penalty of

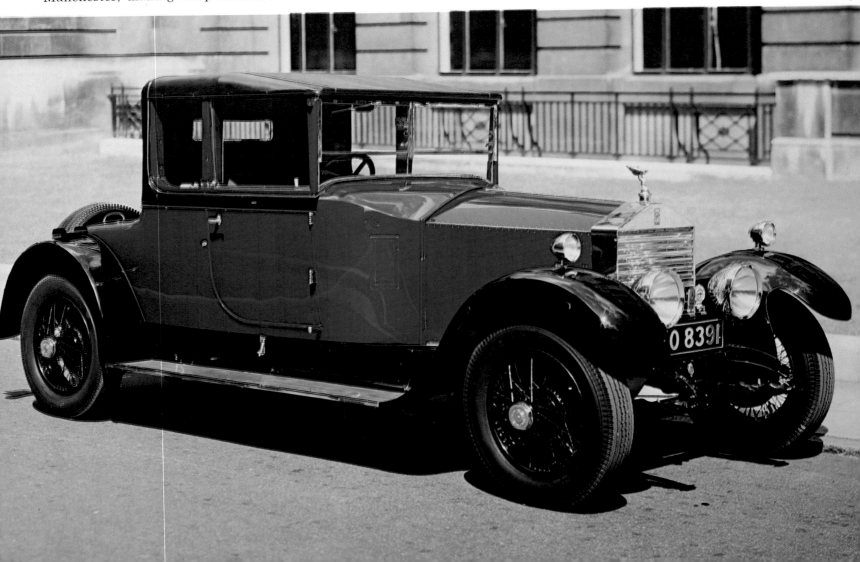

PREVIOUS PAGES: Rolls-Royce Silver Ghosts were made in Springfield, Massachusetts, from 1920 until 1926, and Phantom I's from the following year until the factory closed in 1931.

BELOW: Introduced in 1965, the unitary construction Silver Shadow represented a completely new design (apart from the engine) for Rolls-Royce. The basic specification has altered little since, with the 1960 6,750 cc V8 engine, automatic transmission, all-round independent suspension and power-assisted disc brakes, but like all products from Crewe, Cheshire (where the cars have been made since 1946), it has been gradually improved over the years and is today still one of the finest examples of automobile engineering money can buy. This is a 1976 model in North Africa.

LEFT: Doctor's coupé. A cheaper and smaller 20 hp Rolls-Royce was introduced in 1922 to cater for the "professional" owner.

RIGHT: The 1920 Silver Ghost had a chassis-only price of £2,100. The design was by now a little elderly and the new Phantom was introduced in 1925.

THE AUTOCAR.   ADVERTISEMENTS.   MARCH 30TH, 1907.. 15

THE SIX-CYLINDER
ROLLS-ROYCE

THE 40-50 H.P. SIX-CYLINDER ROLLS-ROYCE DOUBLE LANDAULET.

"The most smooth running petrol car."
—Country Life, December 29th, 1906.

The most luxurious and best appointed car for town or country.

SILENT, VIBRATIONLESS, WONDERFULLY FLEXIBLE, FAST HILL-CLIMBER, RELIABLE, AND ECONOMICAL.

Particulars on application.   Trial by appointment.

ROLLS-ROYCE, Ltd.,
14 & 15, CONDUIT STREET, LONDON, W.

AGENTS for LEICESTER, NOTTINGHAM, RUTLAND, AND DERBYSHIRE . . . .   The Midland Counties Motor Garage Co., Granby Street, Leicester.
AGENTS for NORTH RIDING of YORKSHIRE AND DURHAM . . . .   The Cleveland Car Co., Cleveland Bridge Works, Darlington.
AGENTS, FRANCE . . . . . .   La Société Anonyme " L'Eclaire," 50, Rue la Boétie, Paris.
AGENTS, UNITED STATES of AMERICA . . . . . .   The Rolls-Royce Import Co., Broadway, New York.
Telegrams: "Rolhead, London."   Telephones: 1497/1498 Gerrard.

years of overwork, infrequent snack meals at the work-bench, and an unremitting passion for perfection. From 1911 he was a semi-invalid, but this did not diminish his, or his firm's, capacity. Largely due to the influence of his partner Claude Johnson, Royce agreed to spend most of his time working at home, either in Le Canadel in the south of France or at West Wittering in Sussex.

After the purchase of the bankrupt Bentley company in 1931, Bentley and Rolls-Royce cars were made side by side, with differences only in detail, and for the Bentley more quality and refinement than had been the case in its independent days at Cricklewood. Both cars were made at Derby, where Rolls-Royce had moved in 1908, and after the 1939–45 war a second transfer was made to Crewe, where operations continue to this day.

In 1947, the Phantom III (a twelve-cylinder giant of 7 litres introduced in 1935) was replaced by the first post-war model, the Silver Wraith.

Just 16 straight-eight Phantom IV's were built for heads of state from 1949; one of the distinguished customers was H.R.H. Princess Elizabeth, who by buying a Rolls-Royce broke the English royal family's traditional link with the Daimler factory established in 1900 by Edward VII. Factory-built bodies were introduced

in 1949 (previously, customers had specified their own coachbuilder) on the export-only Silver Dawn. Its successor, the Silver Cloud, acquired a V8 engine in 1960. The Silver Shadow was announced in 1965. It had unitary construction of body with chassis (a radical departure) and self-levelling all-round independent suspension, but retained the classical, Grecian radiator introduced with the first car to bear the name in 1904.

In 1971 the bankruptcy of the parent aero-engine company created a temporary stir; but predictably, it was found that Rolls-Royce motor cars could exist profitably as a separate entity. That year saw the introduction of the Corniche two-door saloon or convertible, and by the end of the year the 10,000th Silver Shadow had left the Crewe factory.

Latest in the line is the Camargue, costing in 1977 more than £40,000, but with a long waiting list of customers. Out of an annual production of about 3,000 cars, ranging from £18,000 upwards, about 1,000 go to America, 130 to the Middle East, and at least 1,200 remain in Britain. The same standards laid down by Frederick Henry Royce are still maintained, the car is still considered by many to be the best in the world, and customers still find that "the quality remains after the price has been forgotten".

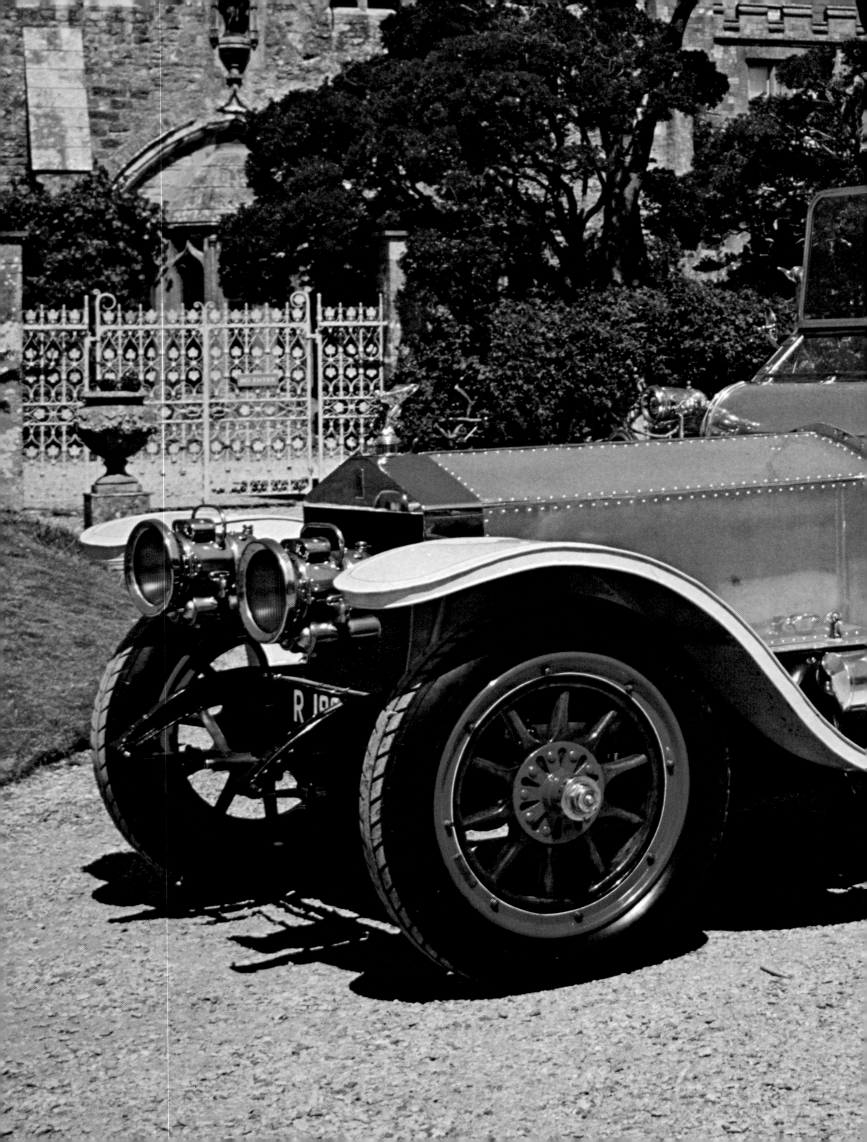

Rolls-Royce Silver Ghost, 1909. The
quintessence of late Edwardian luxury.
INSERT: The Rolls-Royce long stroke 7.4 litre
six cylinder engine, enlarged from 7 litres
in 1909.

LE PUR-SANG DES AUTOMOBILES

Ettore Bugatti was once described as perhaps the greatest maker of racing cars until Enzo Ferrari emerged, and indeed his Type 35 was in the front rank of motor racing for six or seven years, scoring some 2,000 wins between 1924 and 1931. But he also was responsible for a line of road cars of high performance which over the years have become something of a legend for their beautiful, "sculpted" engines and fine design.

Bugatti was born into an artistic Milanese family, but at an early age was attracted by racing, and competed in motor cycling events in northern Italy when only 18 years old.

After a varied career designing cars for Count Gulinelli, Baron de Dietrich, Deutz and Emil Mathis (the latter at Strasbourg) he built the prototype of a small car with a four cylinder engine and shaft drive which was to be the first true Bugatti. Financed with his own money, and constructed in the cellar of his home in Cologne in 1908, this machine is still preserved.

A year later Bugatti found himself a backer and a disused works at Molsheim, near Strasbourg. Car production started. Of advanced design, the first model attracted favourable comment when exhibited at the Paris Salon, competed successfully in speed events, and as the Type 13 had found several hundred customers by 1914. At the end of 1913, the famous horse shoe radiator design was adopted, more pear-shaped than subsequent versions, and said to reflect Ettore's love of horses.

Bugatti's little factory survived the first world war, emerging with French, rather than German, nationality following the return of Alsace-Lorraine to France after the armistice. A bewildering variety of models appeared, all of great beauty but some of uncertain temperament. His designs displayed sparkling originality, sometimes at the expense of essential logic, but it was largely the individuality of his cars, allied to their sporting character, which endeared them to enthusiasts. Wins at Le Mans and Brescia in 1920 and 1921 established the post-war reputation of the company. From 1926 until the end of the decade both racing and sports models were listed in profusion, with the four-seater Type 43, produced between 1926 and 1929, catalogued as the fastest sports car in the world, which with a top speed of 177 km/h (110 mph) it most certainly was.

"Absolute monarch of Molsheim" as

he already was (like Henry Ford, he disliked real titles), Bugatti in 1927 designed the model which was his car for kings, the Royale, Type 41. Of elephantine proportions with a 4.318 m (14 foot 2 inch) wheelbase and propelled by an engine of no less than 12.7 litres, this regal chariot developed 300 bhp and was capable of over 200 km/h (125 mph). Designed to accept the *carrosserie* of the very best coachbuilders in the world, it cost £6,000 in chassis form alone – which is probably why critics called it the "Golden Bug." Guaranteed and maintained free of charge for the life of the owner, it was initially intended that the car should be built in a batch of 25, but in the event only six were completed before the Wall Street Crash of 1929, and of these only three were ever sold (between 1932 and 1933). The white elephant mascot supplied with the Royale proved to be only too apt, although several hundred 5.3 litre (Type 46) were sold as baby Royales from 1930. Such folly would doubtless have ruined any lesser manufacturer, but the Bugatti had acquired a *cachet* of its own long before with other, now revered, models, and in 1931 the Type 51, perhaps the most effective racing car Bugatti ever produced, saved the day.

The dapper little man with the brown bowler hat and Chaplin cane died in 1947, after which serious car production ceased at Molsheim.

In 1977 when the astonishing "secret" Schlumpf collection in eastern France was first discovered, 110 Bugattis were found to be amongst the collection – some of them to be seen for the first time by experts and public alike.

ABOVE: Bugatti built clean and "sculpted" engines – although some of his designs made maintenance a little difficult. This is the power pack of a 1926 2.3 litre Type 35B.

LEFT: Bugatti exotic. The Type 57SC Electron Atlantic coupé, one of Ettore Bugatti's most extravagant designs, was made for just one year, 1937. It housed a 3.2 litre eight cylinder engine.

ASTON MARTIN

Like the Rolls-Royce, the Aston Martin remained faithful to the concept of its creator. Lionel Martin had had successes at the Aston Clinton Hill climb venue with a specially tuned Singer S, and the new car's name celebrated the connection between its creator and the event. Martin believed that the ideal sports car should combine the qualities of a Roll-Royce and a Bugatti, and it is remarkable that most of the products from Newport Pagnell have echoed that sentiment, because Aston Martin history has not been one of unbroken continuity. The company has had no less than five owners since the pre-prototype appeared before the 1914–18 war.

With his partner Robert Bamford, Martin quickly attracted the attention of a wealthy amateur racing driver, Count Louis Zborowski. The cars were beautifully built, held the road like glue, gave 120 km/h (75 mph), in road trim but could be "tweaked" up to about 140 km/h and at such speeds steered with the precision of a watch movement. With financial assistance from the Count, a racing programme was drawn up. A number of racing cars were built, some with experimental twin overhead camshaft engines, and given names like "Bunny", "Razor Blade" (an extremely narrow car) and "Green Pea", but lack of money always dogged the company.

The Depression did not hit Aston Martin as badly as some firms, and between the wars its best production year was in 1933 with 105 delivered to owners,

following a short period during which they were allied to Frazer-Nash. Standards were never compromised, however, and a faithful band of followers was built up throughout the Thirties, with the reputation of the marque enhanced by the winning of the Bienniel Cup at Le Mans in 1932, and a class win in the Mille Miglia in 1935.

After the 1939–45 war, a millionaire tractor manufacturer, David Brown, took over and revitalized the company. The famous DB series evolved, and in 1948 a 2 litre version won the Belgian 24-hour race at Spa in the hands of Jock Horsfall and Leslie Johnson.

From 1950, a 2.6 litre engine, which W. O. Bentley had designed for the old Lagonda company (which David Brown also bought), replaced the 2 litre unit, giving the cars a zero to 100 km/h time of only 12 seconds. Subsequent models did nothing to detract from the charisma of the name, and racing versions scored wins at Nürburgring; at Spa in 1957; first, second and third places in the 1958 T.T.; a first and second at Le Mans in 1959; and finally first place in the Sports Car Constructors Championship (the only British makers to achieve this) the same year.

By 1960, the G.T. short chassis model with the 302 bhp engine was capable of 273 km/h (170 mph). Latterly, V8 engines have been used, although sixes were also offered until 1972. Sporting success has not diminished Aston Martin's financial problems, which have hampered the company's operations, but enthusiasm for the marque will always prevail.

TOP: Few companies can have had more changes of ownership than Aston Martin. Two things, however, have remained consistent: the quality, and the demand from enthusiastic customers. With a 5.4 litre V8 engine which is equally at home in town traffic or at 260 km/h (160 mph), it employs four overhead camshafts and can accelerate from 0 to 160 km/h (100 mph) and back to zero all in less than 20 seconds.

ABOVE: Aston Martin had recently freed themselves from an association with Frazer-Nash when the 1933 1½ litre long chassis model appeared, and R. G. Sutherland (who was to control the company's destinies until the David Brown take-over) was at the helm. Fifth place overall at Le Mans was among the year's achievements. This is the classic front end of the 1933 model.

RIGHT: Rolls-Royce took exception to this case of imitation, and the radiator of the 1913 Sizaire-Berwick was the cause of litigation for infringement by Rolls. The Anglo-French Sizaire-Berwick competed in the luxury market with a degree of success, and was finally taken over by Austin in 1923.

HISPANO-SUIZA

King Alfonso XIII of Spain bought a 20 hp Hispano-Suiza in 1905. When the 1910 Coupe de l' Auto Race was won by the Type 15T, his queen presented him with one, and the model became known as the Alfonso. But with or without royal patronage, success would have come sooner or later: the Hispano-Suiza was an outstandingly well-made car.

The firm had always catered for the carriage trade, but the Alfonso gave impetus to the Hispano-Suiza sporting image, and it became one of the very few Spanish cars ever to make an impression outside Spain. From 1911, a French factory also operated, and it was here during the 1914–18 war that the firm's leading light, the Swiss engineer and designer Marc Birkigt, built his highly successful V8 aero engine. Derived from this, a V12 was planned but never produced, but in 1919 a luxurious touring sports car, with an overhead camshaft six cylinder engine which was virtually one half of the V12, was shown on the Hispano stand at the Paris Salon. Called the H6B, it took the motor world by storm, established the reputation of the French factory, and caused some to question Rolls-Royce's claim to making "the best car in the world."

Exploiting the fame of the aero engine, which had been used in French, British and American aircraft during the war, Birkigt adopted for his cars the stork mascot of George Guynemer's famous fighter squadron, the "Escadrille des Cigognes".

In modified form (and also as the 8 litre 45 hp Boulogne H6C), the H6B was built well into the Thirties, and in 1931 was joined by a new V12. With an engine of 9.5 litres, this was the largest, most expensive and most complex of all the Hispanos; despite pushrod-operated overhead valves, speeds of 185 km/h (115 mph) were possible and all V12s were capable of over 160 km/h. It was available from the factories at Barcelona and Bois Colombes, Seine, until 1938, and its enormous wheelbase attracted bodywork from the best coach-builders of Europe and America. The smaller sixes were built at Barcelona until 1944.

ABOVE: Until 1924 one of the select band of manufacturers who could compete for Rolls-Royce's clients, Napier was at one time one of the most respected marques in the world. In 1907, when this large 60 hp 7.7 litre six cylinder model was made, S. F. Edge was energetically promoting the company and the car and had just succeeded in averaging 106 km/h (66 mph) around Brooklands for 1,582 miles in 24 hours.

The apparent large size of this 1910 Pierce-Arrow is not entirely artist's licence. Only four years later the company were fielding a "six" of some 12.7 litres, and from the time the Arrow had been added to the Pierce name in 1904, size and output had gradually increased.

The Pierce Arrow

THE six-cylinder idea is no more a rightful adjunct of the Pierce-Arrow Car than are a hundred other sound ideas of car construction that we have adopted after a thorough trying out. Luxury means efficiency always.

THE PIERCE-ARROW MOTOR CAR COMPANY, BUFFALO, N.Y.
Licensed under Selden Patent

AUBURN, CORD AND DUESENBERG

While it is usual to consider these three American makes as essentially the same, since they were all eventually produced in Erret Lobban Cord's empire, the Duesenberg was the true thoroughbred of the three and one of the greatest American motor cars of all time. Fred and August Duesenberg had come to America as children with their parents from Germany in the 1880s. The first true car production to bear their name, the Model A, appeared in 1920, but racing cars had been constructed at the Indianapolis works since 1913, and with this pedigree behind them, the Model A was not unnaturally an extremely advanced car. Sharing with the Kenworthy the distinction of being the first American straight eight production car, it was similar to the racing model, and developed 100 bhp.

Hydraulic brakes (another American first), also made the Duesenberg unique at this time, but such refinement could be bought only at tremendous expense and it was not unknown for cars to cost $25,000. This restricted the market, and by 1926 the Duesenberg brothers were in

trouble. Rescue came in the form of Erret Lobban Cord, a colourful ex-racing driver, mechanic and garage operator turned speculator and motor manufacturer. He was already running the Auburn company in Indiana and was later, in 1929, to produce the Cord – the first really successful front-wheel drive American car.

Cord's money financed the Model O, the best-known Duesenberg of all, bigger, faster and more expensive than any other American car. With an eight cylinder, 6.9 litre engine built by Lycoming (which Cord also owned), the huge car (weighing nearly 2,270 kilograms or 5,000 lbs) could manage 187 km/h (116 mph) in top gear and 143 km/h (89 mph) in second, and developed 265 bhp – twice the output of its nearest rival.

In 1932 came the Model SO, even more fabulous than its predecessor, capable of no less than 320 bhp. With acceleration of 0–160 km/h (0–100 mph) in a lightning 17 seconds, and a top speed of 207 km/h (129 mph), the car endeared itself to princes and movie stars alike and, mainly because of its outstanding qualities, Duesenberg weathered the depression. The phenomenon could not live indefinitely. Fred Duesenberg was killed driving one of his cars in 1932 and Cord overreached himself with his other commitments, going bankrupt in 1937. But the Duesenberg did not die. Of the 550 Os and SOs made, no less than half have survived, and replicas are being built by more than one present-day company to satisfy people who cannot afford the real thing. These cars had ultimate snob appeal: *Vanity Fair* advertisements of the Thirties would claim that the aspiring socialite had not "arrived" unless he (or she) drove a Duesenberg.

OTHER GREAT MARQUES

There are, of course, other names with claims to greatness. Daimlers, for instance, have been the cars used by the British royal family for most of the 20th century. Lanchester also aspired to the same position, but upset George V at the 1919 Motor Show. Their six cylinder 40 had a Louis Quatorze appearance, the interior as ornate as the Palace of Versailles. "Very fine, Mr. Lanchester," said the king quietly, "very fine. But more suited to a courtesan than a prince, wouldn't you say?"

In America makes such as Pierce-Arrow, Locomobile and Packard vied with McFarlan, Wills St. Claire and Heine-Velox for the loyalty of the true enthusiast. Duesenberg, however, set the standard in the United States during the Twenties and Thirties, with Cadillac surely a close second: together with Lincoln the latter is now considered the Presidential car *par excellence*.

There is still, fortunately, a market for the very best motor cars that money can buy and the great marque survives today – still select, exotic, luxurious, and very expensive.

FAR LEFT: The 1929 Duesenberg Model J was capable of an astonishing 187 km/h (116 mph). The supercharged SJ appeared in 1932 (this is a 1937 car with LeBaron coachwork) and could go from 0 to 160 km/h (100 mph) in just 17 seconds.

CENTRE: Auburn, Cord and Duesenberg upheld US manufacturing reputation during the Twenties. This is the supercharged Cord 812 of 1937, showing its extremely modern layout.

BELOW: With a front-mounted V8 engine of over 7 litres, the 1977 Cadillac Eldorado is the largest-engined production car in the world, with a top speed of 195 km/h (121 mph).

The Great Race

Less than ten years after Benz and Daimler had created their first shaky cars, the inevitable happened – enthusiasts mounted the first motor sporting event. It was a French occasion, for only in France were the roads good enough, and only in France were there sufficient horseless vehicles in 1894.

The 126 kilometre (78 mile) Paris-to-Rouen Trial was promoted by a newspaper, *Le Petit Journal*, whose editor had been disappointed by a recent journey in a motor vehicle when he had needed to reach the scene of a story before his paper went to press. The car had broken down. M. Giffard decided that a competitive event to encourage the reliability of the horseless carriage would be to the public benefit. This gathering, on a July day at the Porte Maillot in Paris, was not a race but a reliability trial. The winning car was to be the one that was judged "without danger, easily handled, and of low running cost."

However, as soon as the leading vehicle was out of sight of the starting-line, speed entered the contest. There were incidents in plenty, but only four vehicles were actually *hors de combat* at the finish in Rouen. All four were steam-driven, which gave an immediate boost to the petrol-fuelled car. Almost all of the twenty-one participants were inexperienced at fast driving and one, Etienne La Blant, who was to drive a Serpollet steam van, ascended the pavement before the start, demolishing several park seats. He was politely described by the journal as a "person of good intentions but insufficient automobile experience".

A big de Dion steam-car arrived first at Rouen, its occupants hugely enjoying the city's cheering welcome. However, they were disqualified because of the machine's high running costs. The prize of 5,000 francs was finally divided between Messieurs Panhard & Levassor and M. Peugeot, "both employing the petrol engine invented by Herr Daimler of Württemburg". Herr Daimler himself had travelled to the event by train.

BELOW: A Renault won the first French Grand Prix, run in 1906 over a circuit at Le Mans. Hungarian driver Ferenc Szisz won the two-part race at almost 102 km/h (63 mph), helped considerably by his 90 hp car's quick-change detachable wheel rims.

Berlin (1901), Vienna (1902) and, in 1903 to Bordeaux, although the final destination was to have been Madrid.

THE FIRST RACES IN THE U.S.A.

Meanwhile, in North America motor racing had caught the imagination of several rich sportsmen. There had been a dubious event in November 1895 between a small group of creaking and puffing autos sponsored by the *New York Times Herald*, run from Chicago to Evanston, where all but an American Duryea and a Benz were abandoned at the roadside. The first prize was disputed between the Duryea and the Benz.

Genuine racing came to the U.S.A. with the first Vanderbilt Cup. Willie K. Vanderbilt Jr. had raced for a full two seasons in Europe including the capital-to-capital races – he used a massive 70 hp

Next year, 1895, there was a genuine race, from Paris to Bordeaux and back, a total of 1,178 kilometres (732 miles). It was a marathon for such frail vehicles, but some 22 set off. The programme announced "*12 voitures à pétrol, 6 voitures à vapeur* (steam cars), *un électrique,* and *trois cycles à pétrol*". One Peugeot was driven by the brothers Michelin, who had fitted pneumatic tyres previously used on their bicycles, now to be tested under stress.

Emile Levassor's two-seater Panhard powered by the Daimler-designed twin-cylinder four hp unit soon overtook the large steamers and pounded down the dusty roads towards Bordeaux. His co-driver would be waiting for him at Ruffec, near Poitiers, to relieve him for a few hours. Levassor arrived at Ruffec to find the man still in bed. He continued to Bordeaux alone, turned and headed back for Paris. After driving through a second night by the light of his flickering candle-headlights, virtually non-stop 48 hours 48 minutes, he arrived in Paris, some six hours ahead of his nearest rivals. The Marquis de Chasseloup-Laubat, holder of the first motor car speed record, described the victor: "He did not appear overtired . . . we lunched together at Gillet's at the Porte Maillot. He was quite calm; he took with relish a cup of bouillon, a couple of eggs and two glasses of champagne; but he said that racing at night was dangerous, adding that having won he had the right to say such a race was not to be run another time at night."

Levassor's speeds of up to 32 km/h (20 mph) (his average was 24 km/h or 14.91 mph) with virtually non-existent head-

lights qualified him to comment. In fact, he did not win that race, because the regulations stated that only four-seater cars could compete officially, but the victory was Levassor's in all but prize money.

Such was the character of motor racing in the late 19th century: trials of strength – as much of the driver as of his vehicle. Rapid advances in reliability soon introduced international open-road racing, usually starting from Paris, to Marseilles and return (late 1895), Amsterdam and return (1898), Toulouse and return (1897),

ABOVE RIGHT: Flying stones and splashes of hot road-tar were two of the hazards of race-driving in pioneer days. These two American drivers are well-equipped for the dangers of rapid travel.

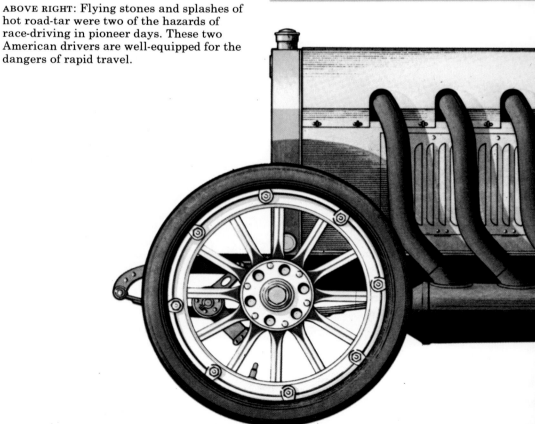

Mors most of the time – and was determined to bring the new sport home.

For the first five years, the series was held over various circuits on Long Island, one of which actually ran through New York City; an ideal venue for New Jersey society, who took the event to heart to the extent of writing a musical named after it. The course was not so idyllic for the competitors: it was cluttered with tramlines, railroad crossing and main street junctions, but only a handful of police officers controlled adjoining roads. Cries of "car coming" were the only safety precautions; spectators would scatter for their lives.

By 1904, the first Vanderbilt year, competition cars were no longer puttering single-cylinder frailties; most were mechanical leviathans. Since the new Mercedes had shocked the motor-racing

ABOVE: The driver of a de Dietrich changes a stripped tyre during the first Grand Prix, held at Le Mans in 1906. Passing the car is the winning Renault, with Hungarian Ferenc Szisz at the wheel. (Painting by Gordon Crosby.)

LEFT: The 1895 Paris to Bordeaux race. Emile Levassor's Panhard waits for the signal to start on the 1,171 kilometres (732 miles) marathon that he was to drive (and unofficially win) single-handed and without a break.

BELOW LEFT: Benz were deeply committed to racing by 1909, usually competing against their arch-rivals Mercedes. This racing Benz was chain driven although passenger vehicles used the more modern propeller shaft. It performed well in the 1908 Grand Prix and by 1909 had entered the contest for the World Speed Record and won. It was to hold the record for 13 years as the Blitzen Benz, during which time its 21.5-litre 200 hp engine was clothed in a streamlined body.

coterie in 1901 with its innovations and by its wins at the Nice Week sporting events, others were now copying the mechanically operated inlet valves, honeycomb cooling and four-speed, sliding gear change, and had gouged out engine blocks until the cylinders were truly enormous.

Entries for the 1904 Vanderbilt race included no less than five Mercedes (four 60 hp, one 90 hp), three large Panhards (aggressive, sharp-edged machines), a 75 hp Fiat, an 80 hp de Dietrich and a similar-sized Clement-Bayard. American-built vehicles included a Pope-Toledo, a Simplex, a 30 Packard Grey Wolf, and the favourite driver, Joe Tracy, in a Royal Tourist. The race developed into a battle between a Panhard and a Clement-Bayard and was, after nearly 480 kilometres (300 miles) of hair-raising driving on the rough course, won by an American, George Heath, in the Panhard at an average of 84 km/h (52.2 mph). As soon as the two leading cars had crossed the line, the race had to be hurriedly stopped because the crowds had nonchalantly begun to wander over the course at the finishing line.

The Autocar branded the event as mismanaged. America's motoring journal, *Horseless Carriage*, called it a "barbarous exhibition for a state marching in the forefront of civilisation". Nonetheless, manufacturers realized that publicity gained by winning an event brought increased sales.

ROAD RACES

Inter-town races, starting with the Paris–Bordeaux event won by Levassor in 1895, were to become the yearly highlights of the European season. The Paris–Berlin race of 1901 had attracted tremendous

publicity and brought in the largest entry of any motor race held to that date. In 1902, a Paris-to-Vienna race was mounted, encompassing another event – the Gordon Bennett Cup, a trophy given annually since 1900 by the eccentric proprietor of the *New York Herald*, James Gordon Bennett, for cars recognized by the Automobile Club de France. The Gordon Bennett race was to be run concurrently, on the same route as the Paris–Vienna event, but finishing at Innsbruck.

A huge entry of 117 cars started at 3.30 a.m. on July 25, Fournier in a 60 hp Mors, a giant of over nine litres which averaged a flying 113 km/h (70 mph) over the first hour. Fournier's flamboyant driving – he had been impressing a trainload of enthusiasts following in a chartered express train – soon had him on the roadside inspecting a ruined gearbox. René de Knyff arrived first at Belfort, the first halt, in his 13.7 litre Panhard.

Next came the Arlberg Pass into Austria. Formidable even today, it presented unspeakable horrors to the motorist of 1902. Its mule-track of a road snaked up into the clouds; it was snow-bound and rutted. So steep was it that some chose to negotiate stretches in reverse gear (the lowest ratio); the surface was so bone-shaking that others lashed their feet to the pedals.

A British driver, Selwyn Edge, won the Gordon Bennett section in a lightweight 6.5 litre Napier after a needle-match with de Knyff's Mors, and a sojourn in a wayside ditch. The Paris–Vienna cars (this larger class had an official weight limit of 1,000 kg, but competitors unofficially pared down their machines, often unsafely, by boring holes in frame and superstructure) hurtled on through Austria to

Salzburg, the penultimate stop. Marcel Renault, brother of Louis and head of the growing empire at Billancourt, was lying seventh in his small 16 hp Renault.

Marcel, lucky enough to be still on the road after 800 kilometres (500 miles) decided to take an all-out gamble on the last section to Vienna. Purposefully driving his open car at 120 km/h (some 75 mph) through the blinding dust clouds thrown up by the leaders he surged through the field. Finally, only Count Zborowski's large 40 hp Mercedes and Farman's Panhard were ahead. They too were overtaken by the 3.7 litre car, which arrived at the Prater in Vienna almost two hours before the winner was expected. The Viennese had expected a Mercedes to be first, and at first refused to believe the early arrival when he protested that it was he, Marcel Renault from France, who had just driven from Paris faster than the multi-horsepower Mors, the great Panhards and the Mercedes, in his *voiture legère*.

TRACK RACING

The following year, 1903, saw the end of city-to-city racing when five competitors, including Marcel Renault, and several of the watching crowd were killed in the notorious Paris–Madrid "Race of Death".

Motor racing had attained such speeds that a move to a closed road circuit, at which protection for the public and competitors could be arranged and supervized, was imperative. The sport demanded it, and the French insisted upon it, mainly, it must be said, as French manufacturers wished to field a greater variety of cars in a sport which until then had restricted them to the same number of entrants as any non-producing country. So the French

Grand Prix (officially the Grand Prix de l'Automobile Club de France) was born.

The first Grand Prix took place in June 1906 on a great triangular circuit at Le Mans in the Sarthe region and was a just victory for a French car, once more a Renault. Driven by a Hungarian, Ferenc Szisz, the 13 litre *bolide* covered 12 laps of the 103.17 km (64.12 mile) circuit at the high average of 101.17 km/h (62.88 mph). For this race, Renault used a new Michelin development, detachable rims ready-fitted with tyres which saved precious time and contributed in no small way to the Renault victory.

Since that first Grand Prix, Formula racing has been governed by regulations or formulae that were and are, para-doxically, designed to restrict perform-ance. One of motor sport's *raisons d'être* is to pass on to the production vehicle lessons learnt in competition, and indeed Grand Prix racing has been prevented from developing along technical lines which could have severed completely its links with the ordinary car.

From 1908 to the present day, the Grand Prix formulae have been:

    1906 Maximum weight 1,000 kg
    1907 Fuel consumption limit 9.4 mpg
    1908 Piston area limited to 117 sq ins (and a 155 mm bore for four-cylinder motors)
    1912 No restrictions (Formula Libre)

TOP LEFT: The streamlined Blitzen Benz of 1911. With four cylinders it provided 200 hp at 1,500 rpm. Driven by American Barney Oldfield it clocked 228 km/h (141.7 mph) at Daytona, setting a world speed record that was not officially recognised. Its 1910 speed of 211.94 km/h (131.72 mph) is the record that stood in the reference book until 1922.

TOP CENTRE: Refuelling during the 1910 Vanderbilt Cup Race at Long Island.

TOP RIGHT: In 1914 the French Grand Prix was won for Germany by the Mercedes team. The cars were the first Mercedes to feature shaft drive and had a maximum speed of about 160 km/h (100 mph).

ABOVE: Opel's record-breaking racing car was developed during 1913 for works entries into racing, and for speed records. Its 260 hp was produced by a four cylinder unit of 12 litres with overhead camshaft and four-speed box.

THE FIRST RALLIES

The Rally Automobile Monte Carlo was dreamed up as a gentler sport than racing, a kind of reliability trial similar to, but considerably longer than, the first Paris to Rouen event. It has also been unkindly said that it was invented to fill empty hotels in January.

In January 1911, from starting points at Paris, Boulogne, Madrid, Rome, Berlin, Vienna, Brussels, Amsterdam, Geneva, Lisbon and St. Petersburg, twenty-three brave crews set off for Monaco. The time allowance for the journey was seven days. At an average speed of around 24 km/h (15 mph), the event was won by M. Henri Rougier in a Turcat Mery.

This gentle sport soon caught on – and other countries joined in with their own rallies. Tests and *Concours d'Elegance* became part of rallying, with marks for arrival at various control points on the route at specified times. Later, special speed trials on short, closed portions of the route changed the character of rallying, bringing its present-day form, a hard, rugged sport, which tests the car, often to destruction, and provides information about current products.

1913 Fuel consumption limit 14.2 mpg

1914 Maximum engine capacity four and a half litres unsupercharged

1921 Maximum engine capacity three litres

1922–1925 Maximum engine capacity two litres

1926–1927 Maximum engine capacity one and a half litres

1928–1933 Free-Formula

1934–1937 750 kilogrammes maximum weight

1938–1939 Maximum capacity three litres supercharged or four and a half litre unsupercharged

1946–1951 Maximum one and a half litres supercharged or four and a half litres unsupercharged

1952–1953 Maximum 500 cc supercharged or two litres unsupercharged

1954–1956 Maximum 750 cc supercharged or two and a half litres unsupercharged (pump fuel compulsory by 1958)

1961–1965 Maximum 750 cc supercharged or one and a half litres unsupercharged

1966 Maximum one and half litres supercharged or three litres unsupercharged

The Grand Prix of 1906 was only one in a rapidly growing list of events. On the Isle of Man in September 1905 a race had been run for touring cars. The island had been chosen after it was found to be the only part of the United Kingdom free from restrictions on competing over public highways. The Tourist Trophy was to become Britain's most historic race and continues today as a motorcycle event, with the car TT at Silverstone.

In Sicily, wealthy Vincenzo Florio had mounted another island race, over rough roads and through bandit-infested country. The roads were negotiable, but Florio had to make several of the *banditti* stewards of the meeting in order to dissuade them from taking pot-shots at the competing cars. The Targa Florio also became one of the world's longest-lived events.

In Germany the following year (1907), a similar race took place when the Kaiser offered a prize for touring cars not exceeding eight litres over a course in the Taunus mountains. Restrictions kept out genuine racing cars, although the Kaiserpreis was in fact the German answer to the French Grand Prix. That year was a classic for Italy's Fiat racing team: a young driver, Felice Nazarro, won all three major races (Grand Prix, Targa Florio and Kaiserpreis).

In July 1907, the first purpose-designed race track, then called an autodrome, was opened at Brooklands near Weybridge in England. It was a two and three-quarter-mile banked circuit given by H. F. Locke-King as a testing ground for the infant motor industry, the development of which was being considerably stunted by the 32 km/h (20 mph) speed limit. The first races, which were run under horse-race rules, attracted few spectators, but when the system of putting up short races on public holidays commenced, Brooklands flourished.

During this period, the French ran another series of races for smaller cars, the *Coupe de l'Auto* or *Coupe de Voiturettes*. Smaller vehicles were soon to eclipse the overgrown and primitive 16 litre dinosaurs, especially when in 1912 the French Grand Prix was convincingly won by Boillot in a 7.6 litre Peugeot. This comparatively tiny car's engine, designed mainly by a Swiss, Ernest Henry, was the foundation of the design of high-performance engines for the next half century. It had twin overhead camshafts in a four cylinder 16 valve unit, giving a hitherto unimagined 130 bhp from less than eight litres. For the two following seasons, Peugeots were seen collecting most of the world's racing trophies and their leading driver, Georges Boillot, the favourite of the crowds.

Boillot scored a second place at Indianapolis in May 1914 driving a smaller version of the car, fitted with an advanced 16 valve, four cylinder three litre engine; by July he was in top form with a new four and a half litre car with streamlined

tail and brakes on all of the four wheels.

The French Grand Prix that took place in 1914 on the Lyons-Givors circuit has its place in motor-racing history because it saw the introduction of team tactics, and proved they could win a race. The race was a victory for the Mercedes team and by implication – national feeling ran high at this time – for Germany herself.

One German driver, Sailer, risked his car in hard competition with Boillot, while Christian Lautenschlager held back. The trick worked: although Sailer fell out with a broken crankshaft, Boillot's Peugeot had been too hard pressed from too early in the race, and Lautenschlager took the flag, followed by two team mates. The race had been very complex because massed starts were not yet made and cars commenced at half-minute intervals. Lautenschlager did not realize he had won until told. One month later, war broke out.

LEFT: Mephistopheles was the name given to the huge 18.155-litre Fiat SB4. It was brought to Brooklands in 1908, where it was victorious against the 20-litre Napier. Its speed at Brooklands was said to be over 193 km/h (120 mph).

ABOVE: The S76 Fiat record car built to take the world speed record from the Blitzen Benz. Its pear-shaped radiator and enormous 5ft-high bonnet covered a 28.362 litre engine of some 300 hp. It clocked a claimed 221.02 km/h (137.37 mph) but this speed was never ratified.

THE MAGIC OF THE SPORTS CAR

Motor sport is a good deal older than the sports car itself. Most of the wealthy enthusiasts who supported the embryo motor industry did so – particularly after the turn of the century – for sporting rather than practical reasons. To them, the motor car was not so much a replacement for the carriage and pair as an exciting, new pastime. If it supplanted anything, this was the steam yacht, and the car inherited initially a jargon which owed as much to the language of the sea as it did to the horse and carriage. No well dressed Edwardian sporting motorist would have been complete without his yachting blazer, brass buttons and peaked cap.

One of the best definitions of the sports car is that it is a hybrid, having some of the romance of the pure racing car, yet practical enough to be used as road transport by the family man. Another definition describes it as ". . . one in which performance takes precedence over carrying capacity".

ORIGINS OF THE BREED

Cars of a truly sporting character first began to emerge during the Edwardian period. Isotta-Fraschini of Italy produced high-performance, single overhead camshaft engines from about 1906, but few other contemporary makes boasted such an advanced specification.

Two competitions held between 1905 and 1911, gave important impetus to the sporting road car. The last Herkomer Trophy event was held in 1907, at which time Prince Henry of Prussia, an enthusiastic competitor and younger brother of the Kaiser, announced that he would sponsor a trophy in 1908 for a touring car event. In fact, it was to be the predecessor of the rally. Regulations were strict, and a comprehensive formula was laid down for competing cars. It stipulated engine cylinder bore, horse power, number of seats and many other details, requiring in fact a breed of car designed specifically for the event.

The "torpedo" body – a neat, streamlined shape, with an unbroken hip line, appeared on the German Horch entries: it was designed to circumvent some of the restrictive rules laid down by the Prince, but represented, probably more by luck than judgment, the prototype of true sports car body design. Other even more important developments were occasioned by the Prince Henry events. In 1910, there appeared a three litre Vauxhall designed by Laurence Pomeroy. Developed from the 1908 20 hp car and capable of only about 80 km/h (50 mph), this was however Vauxhall's first L-head engine and capable of greater performance. By 1913, the Prince Henry Vauxhall, as it became known, had acquired a larger engine and was henceforth known as the 30/98 – or Velox – although the original model was still offered until the outbreak of the 1914–18 war. Very few 30/98s actually found their way into private hands during this pre-war period, primarily because the chassis price (£900) was almost double the price of a Prince Henry.

There were other signs of what was to come. If the Vauxhall flouted convention by using a side valve engine when high performance was generally equated with

overhead valves and overhead camshafts, the new increasing use of aluminium, both in crankcase and piston construction, also brought about the flowering of the sports car after 1918. It is significant that, even in 1914, W. O. Bentley, whose own cars were to play such a prominent role during the 1920's, was using aluminium pistons in the D.F.P. (the French Doriot Flandrin et Parant sold in Britain by the Bentley brothers) he had specially prepared for competition.

AERO ENGINE INFLUENCE

Sophisticated engine designs which resulted from wartime experience, particularly in aeronautics, ensured that the fast tourer, or sports car, developed swiftly in 1919. A great many motor car firms were involved in aero engine design and manufacture during the war and of those who adapted their new knowledge to car design, Hispano-Suiza undoubtedly set a standard with their 37.2 hp model boasting overhead camshaft, powerful four-wheel brakes and extensive use of aluminium in the engine. These specifications became standard for a decade after the Hispano's introduction in 1919.

By 1924, most manufacturers in every price range and in every car-producing country were offering some sporting option, although in many cases this consisted of nothing more than the standard model with lightened chassis, spartan, two-seater bodywork and a pointed tail.

The rise of the sports car in the 1920's is understandable even setting aside the prevalent mood of the period. Country roads were still relatively free from traffic; in 1926 there were a mere 1,300,000 privately-owned vehicles in Britain. With what had been learned in the aeroplane industry about high performance engines and metallurgy, there was also new understanding of the gearbox, pioneered by Bugatti in pre-war days. It was now realized that it need not be a mechanism simply for changing speed, but that with properly spaced ratios, it could be as important an aid to acceleration as the engine itself.

As wartime petrol rationing was relaxed and organized racing started again, sports cars proliferated. Even the staid firm of Clyno offered a sports model, and at Oxford Cecil Kimber developed the M.G. Super Sports from the 1.8 litre Morris Oxford. Between them, firms such as Crouch, G.N., Ballot, Frazer-Nash,

PREVIOUS PAGES: The Cord 810 was built in 1935 to a design by engineer Gordon Buehrig. It was front-wheel driven by a V8 power unit and the body style was perhaps the most advanced ever seen at that date, with wrap-round bumpers, sound insulation, and retractable lights. The 810 was followed by this supercharged 812 in 1937.

BELOW: Designed just prior to the first world war, the shaft-driven 28/95 Mercedes was put into production after the Armistice and was immediately successful. Racing driver Max Sailer drove a supercharged version from the factory to Sicily (with a slight interruption for the sea voyage) and there won the Coppa Florio. Superchargers were thereafter offered on an increasing number of Mercedes models, including those with touring and saloon coachwork as well as the purely sports models. This is a 1924 Sportswagen.

ABOVE: Looking much younger than its 60 odd years, and still capable of showing a clean pair of heels to modern machinery, this Alfonso 15T Hispano-Suiza (the model made its first appearance two years before this 1912 example was built) was one of the finest sports cars in the Edwardian period.

LEFT: The 1911 Prince Henry Vauxhall was developed from the 1908 20 hp car which won the 2,000 Miles Trial of that year. It soon developed a reputation for smooth running, sensitive handling, and flexibility of top gear performance. From this chassis was developed the equally famous Vauxhall 30/98.

Vauxhall Successes

1908	RAC 2,000 Miles Trial	1st	20 hp
1909	Scottish Trials	Gold Medal Winner	20 hp
1909	Brooklands O'Gorman Trophy Race	Winner	20 hp
1910	Brooklands O'Gorman Trophy Race	Winner	20 hp
1911	Russian Reliability Trials	Class win	Prince Henry 3 litres
1913	St. Petersburg Winter Race	1st & 4th	Prince Henry 3 litres
1913	Coupé de l'Auto	4th	Prince Henry 3 litres
1913	Waddington Fells Hill Climb and at Aston Clinton, Shelsley Walsh	F.T.D.	30/98 (debut)
1914	Russian G.P.	2nd	30/98 (debut)
1919	Westcliff Speed Trials	F.T.D.	30/98 (debut)
1920	Gaillon	Class win	30/98 (debut)
1921	Kop hill climb	F.T.D.	30/98 'Rouge et Noir'
	Irondown hill climb	F.T.D.	30/98 'Rouge et Noir'
1922–28	17 firsts and international class Records		Three litre ohc TT
1928	Shelsley Walsh record	48 secs	Mays Vauxhall Villiers supercharged
1930	Shelsley Walsh record	45.4 secs	Mays Vauxhall Villiers supercharged
1931	Shelsley Walsh record	43.6 secs	Mays Vauxhall Villiers supercharged
1933	Shelsley Walsh record	42.4 secs	Mays Vauxhall Villiers supercharged

F.T.D. = fastest time of the day

113

H.E., Eric-Campbell, Eric-Longden, Silver Hawk and many others offered a bewildering choice.

Some race tracks, principally Brooklands, enabled the enthusiastic amateur to enter his car against suitably handicapped competitors under the aegis of proper controlling bodies, and even road sprints became popular until a series of accidents brought the inevitable ban in Britain.

Popular though the sports car was, manufacturers were slow to meet the demands of the serious competition sports driver, concentrating still on lethal, giant hybrids often powered by war surplus aeroplane engines. Among such beasts was the original Chitty-Chitty-Bang-Bang, so-called after a song popular with the Royal Flying Corps and not, as most people believe, after its exhaust note. This car had a four-seater, open body and was powered by a 23 litre Maybach aero-engine in a chain-driven Mercedes chassis. Although the car was regularly driven on the road, the increasing availability of more modestly proportioned sports cars eventually relegated it, and others like it, from the road to the track.

ROMANCE OF THE ROAD

What was the "magic" of the sports car? What did the sports car driver really want from his car? For some, it was the thrill of driving a thoroughbred flat-out down a straight road, with the windscreen folded flat, hair streaming, deafened by the wail of a supercharger and the roar of the exhaust. Or it may have been the test of courage involved in piloting a three-wheeler Morgan over dirt roads at speeds well in excess of 129 km/h (80 mph) or some French cycle-car contraption of wire and cardboard with an engine three times more powerful than necessary.

Whatever the magic was, it is largely the same today; and the sports car generally handles better, and is safer at speed *in the right hands* than a saloon. The competitive attitudes which sheer speed and power promote, must, of course, be confined to track events today, but the enthusiast's joy of being in control of a machine as responsive to skill and understanding as a thoroughbred horse was fully appreciated by those who built them. Ettore Bugatti (when he advertised at all) described his cars as "*le pur-sang des automobiles*" – the thoroughbred.

BOTTOM: One of W. O. Bentley's last models before the take-over by Rolls-Royce, this is the 1930 220 bhp six cylinder 8 litre car, of which just one hundred were made. It was possibly Bentley's best production, but came too late to save the independence of his company.

BELOW: The cyclecar that grew up. Frazer-Nash of the early Twenties traced its lineage to the little chain-driven G. N. cyclecar designed by H. R. Godfrey and Archie Frazer-Nash. Its unique transmission of chains and dog clutches requires considerable driving skill and experience. Here a "chain gang" member of the Vintage Sports Car Club waits "on the handbrake" to be flagged away on a speed event.

portions with perhaps a "monocle" windscreen for the driver only, and a steeply raked steering wheel.

The Mercer, Stutz's greatest rival, dated from even earlier, but was succeeded in 1911 by the immortal type 35 Raceabout, built to the same formula. During the Twenties, both Stutz and Mercer had a change of heart and introduced a car more in keeping with the European tourer. Slightly less spartan but no less sporting was the Kissel Gold Bug (offered only in chrome yellow from 1919) favoured by such figures as Jack Dempsey, the famous boxer.

ABOVE: Every inch the thoroughbred, this 1929 six cylinder Mercedes-Benz 7.1 litre supercharged SSK was the ultimate in motoring at the time. Designed as a sports car with a slow-revving and flexible engine for road work it could equally well be tuned up to Grand Prix power, developing some 225 bhp. The history of this car is studded with race victories and speed records, including the 1929 TT, won by Carraciola, and the German Grand Prix 1931.

TOP: The Lancia Lambda featured integral body/chassis construction. The unusual vertical coil front suspension (which Lancia used until 1963 in certain models) and the large front wheel brakes can clearly be seen here. The first Lancia Lambda was produced in 1922; this is a 1928 car with a four cylinder 2,570 cc engine.

BEARCATS AND GOLD BUGS

In America, the sports car developed on different lines. It has become usual to associate two of the best known American performers, the Stutz Bearcat and the Mercer, with the "Roaring Twenties", racoon skin coats and the hip flask. In fact, the Bearcat was a pre-war product – first produced in 1914 – and by the Twenties was past its peak, although second-hand examples were snapped up by bloods. It followed the classic American formula of the period in having a low slung chassis, minimal bodywork (usually two bucket seats, a petrol tank and little else), a slow-revving engine of large pro-

By the end of the Twenties, economic conditions were becoming unfavourable for the low-production, specialist manufacturer. Although in Europe the decade will be remembered as the era when the open car and the open road – as immortalized by Dornford Yates in *Jonah and Company* – came into their own, there was a tendency towards the end of the period for cars to put on weight and acquire closed bodies – often of wood-and-fabric construction. Inevitably this detracted from the sporting character. Typical of the many cars which shared this fate and gradually became "ordinary" cars were the London-built G.N. and the once fast and noisy Rhode.

LEFT: The White House Crash, Le Mans 1927. A Schneider had taken the notorious bend too fast at night and hit the wall. A following Bentley tried to avoid it, drove into the ditch, and a small French Fasto and another Bentley joined the disaster. Finally the 3 litre Davis/Benjafield Bentley swung broadside into the chaos, limped back into the pits – and went on to win the classic race.

BELOW: Winner of the 1928 Le Mans, and immortalized in supercharged form by the exploits of Sir Henry "Tim" Birkin, the 4½ litre Bentley was capable of remarkable speeds, and in Birkin's hands, raised the 1931 Brooklands lap record to 221.48 km/h (137.96 mph).

"THE GREEN" AND ITS RIVALS

Among the heavier cars, the Bentley, although a complete newcomer in 1919 (like the Hispano, it had an aero-engine background), quickly established itself. The 3 litre model finished second, third and fifth in the 1922 T.T. and as late as 1927 scored a remarkable repeat victory at the Le Mans 24 Hours Race. A Schneider, with Tabourin at the wheel, had taken the infamous White House Corner bend too fast and in darkness, hitting the wall of the farmhouse on the left-hand side of the road, finishing up broadside across the road. Next came Callingham in the 4½ litre Bentley, and seeing the obstruction at the last moment he attempted to avoid it, skidded into the ditch, and was himself thrown onto the road. The following car, a Fasto, narrowly missed him, spun and finished up pointing the way it had come, but at least managed to avoid hitting the other two vehicles.

The second Bentley, with Duller driving, was close behind and, faced with the disaster ahead, swung into the ditch already occupied by Callingham's car. Such was the force of the impact that Callingham was thrown back on to the road. Duller was pitch-forked over a hedge, and his car buried itself in the spot recently vacated by the 4½ litre.

When the British journalist and sportsman Sammy Davis arrived in the 3 litre Bentley, the road was almost completely blocked. Fortunately, however, his sharp eyes detected skid marks and debris ahead, and braking heavily he broadsided into the chaos. Davis's Bentley, least damaged of all the cars, had a twisted chassis, erratic steering, no lights and a battery held only by its leads to the car.

Despite the odds, Davis limped back to the pits, where the battery was roped to the car, a new headlight was fitted, and a damaged wheel was changed. By this time the leading Aries was six laps ahead and everyone thought the outcome of the race a foregone conclusion. It was not. Mechanical trouble later put the Aries out after a thrilling duel with the crippled 3 litre Bentley and, between them, Davis and his co-driver Doctor Benjafield brought home the laurels for the Bentley camp. Sammy Davis went on to co-found the Veteran Car Club in 1930, and became sports editor of the motoring journal *The Autocar*.

Bentley's 4½ litre went on to win yet again at Le Mans in 1928, but by 1931 the marque was in trouble. Napier, out of the car-making business since 1924, tried a rescue operation financed by their aero engine business, but Rolls-Royce stepped in at the last moment with a higher bid. Although the Derby-built Bentleys had some sporting pretensions thereafter, the "fastest lorry" image did not persist.

Equally famous, in Germany and elsewhere, was the line of cars from the Daimler Motevan Gesellschaft of Stuttgart, introduced in the twenties by the Mercedes and its successors the Mercedes-Benz. This commenced with the

RIGHT: Elegant Alfa Romeo: a 2.6 litre
Monza, successor to the 2.3 litre that made
its debut in the 1931 Mille Miglia, the classic
round-Italy race.

24/110/160 K (usually known simply as the K for *Kurz*, i.e. short chassis) which pioneered the supercharger and boasted an engine of 6.25 litres. The K was a fine performer, capable of 160 km/h (100 mph) with no trouble and accelerating from 0–95 km/h (0–60 mph) in under 20 seconds. Its successor, the 6.8 litre S of 1927, bettered this performance with a top speed of 177 km/h (110 mph), and notched 53 racing wins and 17 speed records in 1928 alone. It was followed by the superlative 7.1 litre SS, the SSK and SSKL, a breed so powerful it won the German Grand Prix in 1931. Examples of the SSKL can command £75,000 today.

Italy raced a number of excellent contenders in the sports car field during this vintage period, with Alfa Romeo dominating events from 1926 onwards. Even without the assistance which the company received from Mussolini's government, the single and twin overhead camshaft 1500 cc and 1750 cc models would probably have become world famous, and a replica of the 1750 is even today being made to the original drawings (with Alfa Romeo's blessing) by Leontina of Italy.

Vincenzo Lancia introduced his Lambda in 1922. This car typified the unique position which the marque has enjoyed through the years. Never exceptionally fast, the Lancia Lambda nevertheless represented a radical advance in design, using independent front suspension, four-wheel brakes and integral construction of body and chassis inspired by the principle employed in the rigid, shell-like construction of the hull of a ship. Even the engine was unusual – a very narrow V-4 – the configuration Lancia adhered to for well over 20 years. What it lacked in performance, the Lambda made up in handling and soon acquired a classic reputation.

MAINTAINING THE TRADITION

Hard though the Depression years were for specialist manufacturers, sports car makes fared better than most. In this they had one solid advantage over their competitors who made family cars only – customer loyalty and enthusiasm. Part of the charisma of the sports car is the intense marque loyalty which the best examples promote among those who drive

them. Throughout the 1930s, Europe managed to support a large number of small firms making a variety of sporting machinery to suit even modest pockets, and larger firms like M.G. offered cheaper models for impecunious enthusiasts.

At this time, some cars, like the Vale Special (prospective customers were frightened to death on demonstration runs by its ability to slew round in its own length at great speed without turning over), relied upon special features like low ground clearance or, like the B.S.A. Scout, front wheel drive, for their appeal. Delahaye, a French firm which had been known throughout the Twenties for mundane offerings, went one better than Bentley and developed their truck engine into a first class sports unit which delighted everyone by taking second, third, fourth and fifth places in the 1936 French Sports Car Grand Prix. A completely new concept also flourished briefly, the Anglo-American cross-breeds. These combined the better qualities of British suspension and bodywork with large, slow-revving but flexible American engines. In this category were the Lammas-Graham, Brough Superior, Railton and others.

Although the American Cord, Auburn and Duesenberg are now revered for their classic lines, they were not true sports cars in the accepted sense, and appealed more to film stars and other exotic personages than to skilled, sporting drivers. In France and Germany, small companies competed to produce the most advanced designs, and the Thirties saw rubber suspension, front-wheel drive and every possible engine configuration.

POST-WAR REVIVAL

Inevitably, the outbreak of war in 1939 halted car production generally, but it is a measure of sports car appeal that, within months of V.E. Day in 1945, in Britain they were again rolling off the assembly lines. Virtually all went for export to bolster Britain's economy, and this caused a revival of sports car interest in America. A number of home grown models appeared there, including the Crosley Hotshot built by Powell Crosley, the radio pioneer from Cincinatti; the Muntz Jet, a Cadillac-powered slab-sided design taken over from Frank Kurtis by Earl Muntz, a prominent Evansville businessman, and also some cars in the European style built by Briggs Cunningham at Palm Beach, Florida. Between 1951 and 1955 he was to be seen at the wheel of his Chrysler-engined cars at circuits such as Rheims and Le Mans.

In 1948, Jaguar, who had established a reputation for building "poor men's Bentleys" during the Thirties, impressed the world with their exciting XK 120, a 3.4 litre two-seater with six cylinder overhead camshaft engine. Following their official entry into racing in 1950, and in the hands of drivers of the calibre of Peter Whitehead, Peter Walker, Stirling Moss, Tony Rolt and Duncan Hamilton, Jaguar C and D types won Le Mans in 1951, 1953, 1955, 1956 and 1957, in the last race taking first, second, third, fourth and sixth places. If any

manufacturer set the standard for post-war sports cars it was Jaguar, and when in 1960 the firm graduated through the XK 150 to the E type, it met with no less success and, in final V12 form, the E type survived well into the Seventies.

During the Fifties, when austerity and crippling purchase tax threatened to stifle the sports car specialists, a new form, the kit car, emerged. Of these, the Berkshire-built Buckler and the Lotus Seven were the most successful, although of the two only the Lotus is still in production.

Under the guidance of the talented designer, Colin Chapman, Lotus cars grew from this beginning to their present sophisticated status represented by the Elite, Eclat and mid-engined Esprit. No other make of sports car has scored such an impressive list of competition successes in so relatively short a life.

Austin's answer to the Jaguar XK range was the Austin-Healey, a large, handsome two seater, using initially a hotted-up version of the Austin A90 engine, but the car did not fire public imagination in the same way as the XK.

The Sixties brought another generation of hybrids with American engines like the Gordon-Keeble and Jensen, but the real post-war phenomenon was the mass-produced sports car, mainly in the under 2 litre class. These were typified by M.G., who had established a reputation with their smaller models during the Thirties in the face of competition from Singer

ABOVE: Sir William Lyons always maintained that "SS" stood for just "SS" and had nothing to do with Swallow Sidecars (his first venture) or Swallow Specials. By 1938 the SS 100 3½ litre o.h.v., seen here, owed little to the company's humble beginnings, and offered a genuine 160 km/h (100 mph) for only £445. It was the forerunner of the even more illustrious line of cars to follow after the war when they took the name of Jaguar, dropping the "SS".

RIGHT: The 2 litre rear-engined flat-six Porsche 911 was introduced in 1963, with its similar-bodied companion, the 912, which housed a 1582 cc unit. Today the 911 has a 2687 cc powerpack, whilst the Carrera, the sporting version based on the 911, uses a 3 litre engine.

BELOW RIGHT: First appearing in 1965 in prototype form, the Dino 206 (later re-named the 246) was a rear-engined sports model which went into production in 1967. A transversely mounted V6 originally of two litres, the engine was built for Ferrari by Fiat, and the car was named after Enzo Ferrari's son, who had died in 1956. In updated "308" form, and with 2927 cc engine, the Dino continues in production.

and Morgan, and the Austin-Healey Sprite, powered by up-rated versions of the B.M.C. 948 cc engine.

Luxury sports cars were made by the French firm Facel-Vega, by the early Sixties achieving speeds of up to 217 km/h (135 mph), and also by long-established marques like A.C., whose six cylinder engine had been in production since 1919. Bristol, an offshoot of the aeroplane company, based their 1948 400 on the pre-war B.M.W. 328 – one of the great

sports cars to emerge from Hitler's Germany.

Developed from the earlier 326 and 327, the B.M.W. 328 extracted 80 bhp from what was basically a 2 litre engine, had numerous successes in rallies and trials, scored a class win at Le Mans and in 1940 won the Mille Miglia, the 1,000-mile round-Italy race. Its classic shape and styling endeared it to enthusiasts in Britain, where it was marketed as the Frazer-Nash-B.M.W. Frazer Nash had previously been known for their spartan, chain-driven G.N.-based sports cars. Ferrari, who were serious producers only from 1946, emerged as world beaters, both on the road and on the race track.

POST-WAR AMERICA

America's contribution to post-war sports car manufacture has been sporadic. Introduced in the mid-fifties as a "personal car," Ford's Thunderbird was the first noteworthy post-war American sports car. A two-seater initially capable of 182 km/h (113 mph), it was later over-weighted, and ended as a hefty, five-seater convertible with unitary construction of chassis and body. Over-weighting and de-tuning also overtook Ford's Mustang and Shelby series, the result of safety and emission control legislation. Despite Ralph Nader's campaign for safety standards – "Unsafe at any speed" – the Chevrolet Corvette after a shaky start, largely replaced the Thunderbird in the affections of American enthusiasts, and remains faithful to its original concept even after a production run of well over 20 years.

Apparently untouched by events, Morgan alone continues building sports cars of the pre-war type at the rate of about ten per week in a tiny factory in the Malvern Hills, Worcestershire. Their largest offering, the Plus 8, uses a Rover 3.5 litre engine sandwiched into a small chassis which incorporates features which were new in 1910. With this exception, the trend today is towards greater luxury and sophistication. Manufacturers offer cars with the grand touring image, many with closed coupé or saloon rather than convertible bodies.

Typical of this breed is the splendid Porsche 911 series, finely engineered and very fast two-seaters in the super-luxury class. The most costly versions, with a top speed of about 257 km/h (160 mph), incorporate (without loss of good looks) 8 km/h bumpers and other safety features, combined with superb handling. It is, however, a sign of the times that the 924 model has forsaken the noisy, air-cooled Volkswagen-based engine for a front-mounted, water-cooled unit. Despite the option of automatic transmission on some models, and a preoccupation with delicate interior temperature control, the Porsche is no "soft" car in performance terms. It is described (amongst other superlatives) as "the safest production car on the road" and it is true that very few drivers experience handling trouble at or below its top speed.

Museums in Great Britain

The Shuttleworth Collection Old Warden Aerodrome, Biggleswade, Beds. Telephone: Northill (076 727) 288.
Exhibits: Europe's only full range of flyable historic aeroplanes dating from 1909 to the last decade. 28 usually on display as well as veteran cars, bicycles, fire engines, carriages; equipment; library. Flying days are usually the last Sunday in each summer month and on Bank Holidays.

North of England Open Air Museum Beamish Hall, Stanley, Co. Durham. Telephone: Stanley (0207) 33580 and 33586
Exhibits: This 200 acre open air museum re-creates a picture of life in the North East as it was about 1900 and includes most aspects of the history of the North, except for ship-building. Particular reference is paid to the history of railways and road transport.

The Leyland Collection of Historic Vehicles, Donington Park, Castle Donington, Derby.

Exhibits: Selected vehicles from British motor manufacturing companies that over the years were grouped together to form what is now British Leyland, form a unique collection representing different periods, including Albion, Austin, Bean, Daimler, Guy, Jaguar, Lanchester, Leyland, MG, Morris, Riley, Rover, Standard, Triumph, Thorneycroft, Wolseley and others.

The Donington Collection Donington Park, Castle Donington, Derby DE7 5RP. Telephone: Derby 810048
Exhibits: The Donington Collection of single seater racing cars is the world's largest collection of racing cars and has on display over 70 different models from some of the earliest to the latest championship single seater racing cars. The Collection is housed in modern purpose-built accommodation with its own cafeteria, and each car has been immaculately restored to its original condition by the Collection's workshop.

Totnes Motor Museum Totnes, Devon
Exhibits: The main theme of Totnes Motor Museum is mobility. Of the 24 cars usually on display some 15 are in regular use both for everday travel and for racing. The cars form a private collection covering an age span of 50 years and should bring nostalgia and pleasure to all visitors.

Royal Armoured Corps Tank Museum Bovington Camp, Wareham, Dorset. Telephone: Bindon Abbey 721 Ext. 463
Exhibits: Armoured fighting vehicles dating from both World Wars, including tanks, armoured cars, motor cycle combinations, items of equipment, engines, accessories and photographs.

Chipping Campden Car Collection (Incorporated with Woolstaplers Hall Museum) High

Street, Chipping Campden, Glos. Telephone: Evesham 840289 or 840761
Exhibits: The cars exhibited include an 8 cylinder Le Mans Alfa Romeo, a Type 44 and a Type 46 Bugatti, a 1924 Delaunay-Belleville, and 1929 versions of both the Lancia Lambda and Dilambda models.

Gangbridge Collection Gangbridge House, St. Mary Bourne, Hants. Telephone: St. Mary Bourne 220
Exhibits: A collection of 40 motor cycles dating from 1909 to 1965. About 30 have been restored and are in running order. Also three vintage cars (one of which, a G.P. Sunbeam, is normally on loan to the Donington Collection).

National Motor Museum Beaulieu, Hants. Telephone: 0590 612345
Exhibits: This world-famous collection includes more than 200 Veteran, Vintage and post-1930 cars as well as motor cycles, commercial vehicles and four world's land speed record cars. These together with special displays of equipment etc. tell the story of motoring from 1895 to the present day.

Hull Transport Museum 36 High Street, Kingston-upon-Hull, Humberside. Telephone: Hull 27625
Exhibits: Horse drawn vehicles, cars, motor cycles, cycles, trams and railway engines.

Stanford Hall Motorcycle and Car Museum Lutterworth, Leicester. Telephone: Swinford 250
Exhibits: Considered to be the most important collection of historic racing motor cycles in the world. Various other motor cycles are on display and more motor cycles and pedal cycles are to be found in the general transport section (to demonstrate progress in the design), where the accent is on cars.

London General Cab Company Museum 1–3 Brixton Road, Brixton, London SW9. Telephone: 01-735 7777
Exhibits: Historic, prototype and current taxis since 1907 are on display in this small museum.

The London Transport Collection Syon Park, Brentford. Telephone: 01-560 0882
Exhibits: The collection of vehicles can be seen under one roof in company with nearly eighty colourful and historic posters, many photographs and signs, models, tickets and other exhibits.

Science Museum Exhibition Road, South Kensington, London SW1. Telephone: 01-589 6371
Exhibits: The Transport Collection is one of the most comprehensive in the U.K., ranging from bicycles to space craft.

World of Motoring Exhibition Syon Park, Brentford IW8 8JF. Telephone: 01-560 0946
Exhibits: A series of montages covering periods of time, vehicles and motor cycles. There is also a military montage. Part of the exhibition is devoted to varied changing exhibits. These displays are altered every two to three months.

Merseyside County Museum William Brown Street, Liverpool 3, Merseyside. Telephone: 051-207 0001
Exhibits: Transport gallery contains road and rail vehicles.

Caister Castle Museum Caister on Sea, Nr. Gt. Yarmouth, Norfolk. Telephone: 057-284 251
Exhibits: Many vehicles from 1896 to recent times – steam, veteran and vintage, Edwardian etc.

Sandringham Museums Sandringham Estate, Norfolk. Telephone: King's Lynn 2675
Exhibits: The Sandringham Motor Museum forms part of a general Museum Complex and houses a collection of Daimler cars used by various members of the Royal family since Edward VII.

Cheddar Motor Museum Cheddar, Somerset. Telephone: Cheddar 742446
Exhibits: Collection contains 25 veteran and vintage cars and fifteen motor cycles dating from 1898, including a 1903 White Steam Car. There is much motoring miscellany from a bygone age.

East Anglia Transport Museum Chapel Road, Carlton Colville, Lowestoft, Suffolk.
Exhibits: A collection of various forms of land transport collected and gradually being restored to working order by a voluntary society.

The Transport Trust Library at the University of Surrey Guildford, Surrey. Telephone: Guildford 71281 Ext. 328
Exhibits: The Library consists of a large collection of documents, books, journals, photographs, drawings and other archival material connected with all forms and methods of transport.

Weybridge Museum Church Street, Weybridge, Surrey. Telephone: Weybridge 43573
Exhibits: Models, photographs etc. concerned with motor racing and flying at Brooklands, Pennyfarthing bicycle.

Heathfield Wildlife Park Hailsham Road, Old Heathfield, East Sussex. Telephone: Heathfield 4656
Exhibits: Vintage cars and carriages including 1911 Silver Ghost, 1926 Phantom I (previous owner Rudyard Kipling) plus many others. Also special cars, Chitty-Chitty-Bang-Bang (from the film of the same name) and Fab 1 (from the T.V. series *Thunderbirds*) all in working condition.

Herbert Art Gallery and Museum Jordan Well, Coventry, Warwicks. Telephone: Coventry 25555
Exhibits: Transport items connected primarily with Coventry, the "home" of the motor industry. The industrial collection includes 170 cycles, 46 motor cycles and 73 cars and commercial vehicles, as well as aircraft models and engines.

Museum of Science and Industry Newhall Street, Birmingham, West Midlands. Telephone: 021-236 1022
Exhibits: A wide variety of motor cars, motor cycles and bicycles, as well as a Spitfire and Hurricane aircraft.

Stratford Motor Museum 1 Shakespeare Street, Stratford-on-Avon, Warwicks. Telephone: 69413
Exhibits: An ever-changing collection of exotic touring cars including Rolls-Royce Silver Ghost, P2 and P1, Mercedes-Benz 38/250; Hispano-Suiza, Bugatti etc. Many once owned by Indian Maharajahs. Interesting collection of motor cycles, Flying Flea and replica Twenties garage. Picture gallery, motoring books and souvenir shop.

Bradford Industrial Museum Moorside Mills, Moorside Road, Bradford, W. Yorks. Telephone: Bradford 638068
Exhibits: Road vehicles, including loan items: early bicycles and cars.

Jersey Motor Museum St. Peter's Village, Jersey, Channel Isles. Telephone: Jersey (0534) 82966
Exhibits: An interesting collection of motor

vehicles from the early 1900s onwards including vintage Bentleys, a Rolls-Royce Phantom III used in the war by Field Marshal Montgomery and General Karl Spaatz of U.S.A.F., motorcycles, allied and German military vehicles, aero engines, Jersey steam railway relics, lamp and accessory displays, etc.

Man Motor Museum Crosby, Isle of Man. Telephone: 062-485 236
Exhibits: A collection of about thirty vehicles with three or more wheels ranging from an early steamer via the only make of five-wheeled car to a varied selection of Bentleys and Rolls-Royces.

Doune Motor Museum Carse of Cambus, Doune, Central Scotland. Telephone: Doune (0786-84) 203
Exhibits: Lord Moray's unique collection of vintage and post-vintage thoroughbred cars including Hispano-Suizas, Alfa-Romeos, Aston Martins, Bentleys, a Bugatti, Maseratis, M.G.'s, Rolls-Royces, and an Invicta.

Myreton Motor Museum Aberlady, Lothian, Scotland. Telephone: Aberlady 288
Exhibits: Over 70 cars, commercial and military vehicles from a Buick hearse to a Cooper racing car, from a 1922 8.3 hp Renault to a 1920 40 hp Lanchester. Motor cycles from a 1919 Autoped to a Rex Acme sprint cycle, bicycles from 1866 to 1938. Tractors, farm machinery, carriages, very rare aircraft engines from a 1910 Darracq to a 1927 348 cc ABC.

Glasgow Museum of Transport 25 Albert Drive, Glasgow. Telephone: 041-423 8000
Exhibits: The story of the development of the motor car is told with the aid of a considerable collection of Victorian vintage and more modern cars.

Pembrokeshire Motor Museum Garrison Theatre, Pembroke Dock, Dyfed. Telephone: Pembroke 3279
Exhibits: Cycles, motor cycles, H.G.V.'s and cars from 1860 including accessories, clothing tools etc. Wheelwright's tools and shop. Early tractor and exhibits outside.

LEFT: National Motor Museum at Beaulieu, Hampshire.
BELOW: Chitty-Chitty-Bang-Bang at Heathfield Wildlife Park.

AUSTRIA
Technisches Museum für Industrie und Gewerbe
Mariahilferstrasse 212, 1140 Vienna
Heeresgeschichtliches Museum
The Arsenal, Vienna 3
Rennmaschinen-Sammlung Brandstetter
Brunngasse 23, St. Polten
Werksmuseum der Steyr-Daimler-Puch A.g.
Schonauerstrasse, Steyr
Sammlung Ernst Schneidhofer
Bruck a.d. Mur (Steiermark)

BELGIUM
Ghislain Mahy Collection
11, St. Pietersnieuwstraat, 9000 Gent
Historical Automobile Press Information Center
Elyseese Velden 12, 9000 Gent
Provincial Automuseum Houthalen
Kelchterhoef, 3530 Houthalen
Olivier Herbosch Sammlung
Drie Eikenstraat, Antwerpen

CZECHOSLOVAKIA
Narodni Technicke Museum Upraze
Kosteini 42, Prague 7
Tatra Technicke Museum
Koprivnice

DENMARK
Aalholm Automobil Museum
5880 Nysted, near Nykobing F., Lolland
Danmarks Tekniske Museum
Nordre Strandvej 27, 3000 Helsingor
Det Jyske Automobilmuseum

8883 Gjern, near Silkeborg
Egeskovmuseet
Egeskov, near Odense
Trafik-Historisk-Museum
Petershvile, near Helsingor

FRANCE
Autobiographie Renault
Avenue des Champs Elysée, Paris
Autorama Delagrange
D 94, Yerres, Essonne
Conservatoire National des Arts et Métiers
292 rue Saint-Martin, Paris 3
Museon di Rodo
3 bis, Route de Nîmes, Uzès, Gard

Museums in Europe
❦

Musée de l'Automobile de Rochetaillée-sur-Saône
Château de Rochetaillée-sur-Saône, Rhône
Musée de l'Abbatiale
Le Bec-Hellouin 27, Eure
Musée de la Moto et du Velo
Lunéville, Meurthe-et-Moselle
Musée Automobile du Val de Wire
RN 7, Briare, Loiret
Berliet Museum
Vénissieux, Rhône
Musée d'Automobiles de Normandie
D 6, Clères
Musée d'Automobiles du Forez
D 105, Sury-le-Comtal, Loire
Musée Automobile de Bretagne
Route de Fougères, Rennes, Ille-et-Vilaine
Musée de l'Automobile du Mans
Circuit Permanent de la Sarthe, Le Mans, Sarthe
Musée de l'Automobile de Vatan
Total Service Station, RN 20, Vatan, Indre
Musée Bonnal-Renaulac
80 rue Ferdinand-Buisson, Bègles, Gironde
Musée National de la Voiture et du Tourisme
Château de Complègne, Oise
Musée Automobile de Provence
RN 7, 13 Orgon, Vaucluse
Musée Automobile de la Côte d'Argent
Avenue de la Grande Dune, 40150 Mossegoiz
Autorama Musée de l'Automobile
Yerres (Essonne)
Auberg Musée Automobile et Techniques
Petit Arran, Parly (Yonne)
Le Musée
Place de l'Hotel de Ville, Molsheim

*Association des Amis de l'Histoire de l'Auto-
mobile*
49 Rue Petit, Paris
Musée des Voitures
Château de Versailles, Versailles
Musée de l'Antologie Automobile
Villiers-en-Lieu, Saint-Dizier (Hte Marne)

GERMAN FEDERAL REPUBLIC
Deutsches Vergaser Museum
Solex Vergaser, Heidestrasse 52, 1 Berlin 21
Daimler-Benz Museum
Stuttgart-Unterturkheim, Postfach 202
Deutsches Zweiradmuseum
Urbanstrasse 7107, Necharsulm
MAN-Museum
Dachauer Str. 667, Postfach 500620, 8000
Munich
Klockner-Humboldt-Deutz AG Engine Museum
Deutz-Mulheimer Strasse, Postfach 210640,
5000 Köln-Deutz
*Deutsches Museum von Meisterwerken der
Naturwisschenschaft und Technik*
Museumsinsel 1, 8000 Munich
BMW Museum
Lerchenauerstrasse 76, 8000 Munich,
Postfach 400240
Automuseum Nettelstedt
Rietkampstrasse 415, Nettelstedt 4991
Auto-Museum L. L. Hillers
2071 Tremsbuttel bei Bargteheide
Auto Motorrad Museum
Weserstrasse 142, 497 Bad Oeynhausen
Werkmuseum Karlsruhe
Werderstrasse 63, 7500 Karlsruhe
Deutsches Automuseum
Schloss Langenburg, 7501 Langenburg
Sammlung Gut Hand
Hander weg, 5105 Laurensberg
Fahrzeugmuseum Marxzell
7501 Marxzell
Dr. Porsche Sammlung
Porschestrasse 42, 700 Stuttgart-Zuffen-
hausen
Logistikschule der Bundeswehr
Hamburg
Rheinstahl Hanomag AG
Hanomagstrasse 9, Hannover Linden
Schloss Museum auf Hellenstein
Heinenheim
Grenzschutzschule für Kraftfahrwesen
Lübeck St. Huberus
Verkehrsmuseum Nurnberg
Nuremberg
Adam Opel Ag
Russelsheim
Sammlung der Berliner Verkehrs Betriebe
Postdamer Strasse 188, Berlin 30
Verkehrsmuseum Berlin
Hallesches Ufer 74, Berlin 61
Sammlung von Wolfgang Schrunder
Aldruper Weg 39, Greven

HOLLAND
National Automobile Museum
Veursestraatweg 280, Leidschendam
Lips Automobilmuseum
Drunen, Grotestrand 67
National Rutuigmuseum
Nienoord, Leek
De Klinze
Oudkerk
Teewieler Museum
Oudeschoot, Heerenveen

ITALY
*Museo Nazionale della Scienza e della Tecnica
Leonardo da Vinci*
Via San Vittore 21, Milan
*Museo dell'Automobile Carlo Biscaretti di
Ruffia*
Corso Unita d'Italia 40, Turin
Collezione Quattroruote
Rozzano, Milan
Museo Alfa Romeo
Arese, Milan
Museo Lancia
Via S. Paolo, Turin
Museo dell'Automobile
S. Martino en Rio
Centro Storico Fiat
Via Chiabrera 20, 10100 Turin
Pininfarina
Grugliasco, Turin
Padiglione Automobile d'Epoca
Autodromo di Monza, 13054 Monza

MONTE CARLO
Collection de Prince Rainier
Monte Carlo

SPAIN
Museo del Ejército
c/Mendez Nuñez No. 1, Madrid 14
Museo del Automovil de Salvador Claret
Hostal del Rolls, Sils, Gerona
Hotel Rosamar
Lloret del Mar

SWITZERLAND
Musée de l'Automobile
Château de Grandson, Lake Neuchatel, Vaud
Verkehrshaus der Schweiz
Lidostrasse 5, 6006 Lucerne
Feuerwehrmuseum Basel
Kornhausgasse 18, Basle
Collection Augustoni
Via Bossi 6, 6830 Chiasso

Zweirad-Museum
Garage Edy Buhler, 8633 Wolfhausen, Zurich
Sammlung von Prof. Jean Tua
3 rue Pestalozza, Geneva
Musée de Histoire des Science
128 rue de Lausanne, Geneva
Sammlung Hilti
Kirchgasse 43, 9202 Gossau
Collection Strinati
Cours de Rive 3, 1200 Geneva

ABOVE: A stroll down the Champs Elysée in
Paris can lead the enthusiast to the small
but fascinating Renault museum.

LEFT: Bugatti amongst Mercedes – the
Daimler-Benz Museum in the company's
offices at Unterturkheim, Stuttgart.

Museums in the USA

ARKANSAS
The Museum of Automobiles
Route 3, Petit Jean Mountain, Morriton, Arkansas 72110

CALIFORNIA
The Jack Passey Jr. Collection
2025 Freedom Boulevard, Freedom, Cal. 95019
Miller's Horse and Buggy Ranch
9425 Yosemite Boulevard, Modesto
Briggs Cunningham Automotive Museum
250 E. Baker Street, Costa Mesa, Cal. 92626
Los Angeles County Museum of Natural History
Exposition Park, 900 Exposition Blvd., Los Angeles, Cal. 9000
Movieland Cars of the Stars
6920 Orangethorpe Ave., Buena Park, Cal. 90620

COLORADO
Rippey's Veteran Car Museum
2030 South Cherokee Street, Denver, Col. 80202
Forney Transportation Museum
Valley Highway & Speer Blvd., P.O. Box 176, Fort Collins, Col. 80202
Buckskin Joe's Antique Auto Museum
Canon City

CONNECTICUT
Antique Auto Museum
Slater Street, at Interstate 84, P.O. Box 430, Manchester, Conn. 06040

DELAWARE
The Magic Age of Steam
P.O. Box 127, Yorklyn, Del. 19736

DISTRICT OF COLUMBIA
Museum of History and Technology
Smithsonian Institute, Washington D.C. 20560

FLORIDA
Belim Cars of Yesterday
5500 North Tamiami Trail, Sarasota, Flo. 33580
Museum of Speed
Highway 1, South Daytona

Early American Museum
Silver Springs, P.O. Box 188, Flo. 32688
Elliott Museum
Hutchinson Island, Jensen Beach, Flo. 33451
Martin County Historical Society Elliott Museum
888 N.E. MacArthur Blvd., Stuart, Flo. 33494

GEORGIA
Stone Mountain Antique Auto and Music Museum
2042 Young Road, Stone Mountain, Ga. 30083

HAWAII
Automotive Museum of the Pacific
197 Sand Island Road, Honolulu, Haw. 96819

ILLINOIS
Museum of Science and Industry
57th Street & South Lake Shore Drive, Jackson Park, Chicago, Ill. 60637
Fagan's Antique and Classic Automobile Museum
162nd and Claremont Avenue, Markham
The Time Was Village Museum
1325 Burlington Street, Mendota, Ill. 61342
Durward E. Fagan
12043 70th Avenue, Palos Heights
Chicago Historical Antique Automobile Museum
3160 Skokie Valley Road, Highland Park, Ill. 60055

INDIANA
Henry H. Blommel Historical Auto Collection
Route 5, Connersville
Goodwin Museum
200 South Main Street, Frankfort
Elwood Haynes Museum
1915 South Webster Street, Kokomo, Ind. 46901
Indianapolis Motor Speedway Museum
4790 West 16th Street, Indianapolis, Ind. 46224
Early Wheels Museum
817 Wabash Avenue, Terre Haute, Ind. 47808

KANSAS
Abilene Auto Museum
Abilene Center, Abilene
Kansas State Historical Museum
Memorial Building, 10th and Jackson, Topeka

KENTUCKY
Calvert Auto Museum
P.O. Box 245, Calvert City, Kentucky 42029

MAINE
Boothbay Railway Museum
Route 27, P.O. Box 123, Boothbay, Maine 04537

MARYLAND
Fire Museum of Maryland
1301 York Road, Lutherville, Md. 21093

MASSACHUSETTS
Heritage Plantation of Sandwich
Grove and Pine Street, P.O. Box 566, Sandwich, Mass. 02563
Museum of Transportation
Larz Anderson Park, 15 Newton Street, Brookline, Mass. 02146
Sturbridge Auto Museum
Old Sturbridge Village, Route 20, Sturbridge,

P.O. Box 486, Mass. 01566
Edaville Railroad Museum
South Carver, P.O. Box 7, Mass. 02566

MICHIGAN
Henry Ford Museum
Dearborn, Mich. 48121
Sloan Panorama of Transportation
1221 E. Kearsley Street, Flint, Mich. 48503
Woodland Cars of Yesteryear
6504 28th Street S.E., Grand Rapids
Gilmore Car Museum
Hickory Corners
Detroit Historical Museum
5401 Woodward Ave., Kirby, Detroit, Mich. 48202
Poll Museum
353 E. 6th St., Holland, Mich. 49423

MINNESOTA
Hemp Old Vehicle Museum
P.O. Box 851, Country Club Road, Rochester, Minn. 55901

MISSOURI
Kelsey's Antique Cars
Highway 54, P.O. Box 564, Camdenton, Mo. 65020
Autos of Yesteryear
Highway 63, North Rolla, Mo. 65401
National Museum of Transport
3013 Barrets Station Road, St. Louis, Mo. 63122

MONTANA
Montana Historical Society
225 N. Roberts St., Helena, Mont. 59601

NEBRASKA
Hastings Museum
Highway 281 and 14th Street, Hastings, Nebr. 68901
Sawyer's Sandhills Museum
440 Valentine Street, Valentine, Nebr. 69201
Harold Warp Pioneer Village
Highways 6 and 34, Minden, Nebr. 68959
Stuhr Museum of the Prairie Pioneer
Highways 281 and 34 Junction, Grand Island, Nebr. 68801

NEVADA
Harrah's Automobile Collection
Reno, P.O. Box 10, Nev. 89504

NEW HAMPSHIRE
Meredith Auto Museum
P.O. Box 86, Route 3, Meredith, N. Hamp. 03253

NEW JERSEY
Roaring 20s Autos
R.D. 1, Box 178-G, Wall, NJ 07719

NEW YORK
Long Island Automotive Museum
Meadow Spring, Glencove, N.Y. 11542
Golden Age Auto Museum
c/o Timothy O'Connell, 30 Shultze Street, Canajoharie, N.Y. 13317
Upstate Auto Museum
Route 20, Bridgewater, N.Y. 13313
Old Rhinebeck Aerodrome
P.O. Box 57, Rhinebeck, N.Y. 12572

NORTH CAROLINA
Frontier Village
Highway 321, Blowing Rock
Estes Winn Memorial Museum
c/o Biltmore Industries Inc., P.O. Box 6854, Asheville, N.C. 28806

OHIO
Allen County Museum
620 West Market Street, Lima, Ohio 45801
Frederick C. Crawford Auto-Aviation Museum
10825 East Blvd., University Circle, Cleveland, Ohio 44106
Thompson Products
Chester Avenue and East 30th, Cleveland

OKLAHOMA
Horseless Carriage Unlimited
P.O. Box 1887, Muskogee, Okla. 74401

PENNSYLVANIA
Gene Zimmermann's Automobilorama
Holiday West, Route 15, Harrisburg (P.O. Box 1855) Pa. 17105
Swigart Museum
Museum Park, Route 22, P.O. Box 214, Huntingdon, Pa. 16652
Boyertown Museum of Historic Vehicles
Warwick and Laurel Streets, P.O. Box 30, Boyerton, Pa. 1951
Pollock Auto Showcase
P.O. Box 248, Downingtown, Pa. 19335

SOUTH CAROLINA
Joe Weatherly Stock Car Museum
P.O. Box 500, Darlington Raceway, Darlington, S. C. 29532
Wings and Wheels
P.O. Box 93, Santee, S. C. 29142

SOUTH DAKOTA
Pioneer Auto Museum
Highway 16 and 83, Murdo, S. Dak. 57550
Cox's Car Museum

Horseless Carriage Museum
Keystone Route, P.O. Box 255, Rapid City, S. Dak. 57701

TENNESSEE
Old Car Museum
Dixie Gun Works Inc., Highway 51 South, Union City
Smoky Mountain Car Museum
Highway 441, Pigeon Forge
P.O. Box 253, Gatlisburg, Tenn. 37730

TEXAS
Pate Museum of Transportation
Highway 377, Cresson, Texas 76101
Classic Car Showcase
P.O. Box 22592, Houston, Texas 77027

VERMONT
Steamtown U.S.A.
Bellows Falls

VIRGINIA
Car and Carriage Caravan
P.O. Box 748, Luray Caverns, Va. 22835
Roaring Twenties Antique Car Museum
Route 230, Hood, Va. 22723

WISCONSIN
Four Wheel Drive Museum and Historical Building
F.W.D. Corporation, Clintonville
Brooks Stevens Automotive Museum
10325 N. Port Washington Road, 13-W Mequon, Wis. 53092
Sunflower Museum of Antique Cars
Sunflower Lodge, Lake Tomahawk
Berman's Auto and Antique Museum
Highway 14, Oregon

ABOVE: The United States has many fine motor museums, of which the Briggs Cunningham Automotive Museum is probably one of the most interesting. A former car builder and racing driver – his great ambition was to win at Le Mans – Cunningham's passion for collecting cars resulted in his opening a 100-car museum at Costa Mesa, California. Opened in 1966 it houses several of his own sports-racing models, a number of other Le Mans competition cars and vehicles of the past.

Motoring Milestones

1769 The Paris Arsenal, under the direction of the Commandant of Artillery, is authorized by the French government to construct a steam gun-carriage to the designs of Nicholas-Joseph Cugnot. Tested in 1770 it carried four people at 2½ mph.

1801 Cornishman Richard Trevithick's steam road locomotive climbs Camborne Beacon on Christmas Eve, with eight passengers aboard.

1805 The "Drukter Amphibolos" (snorting swimmer), a steam dredger built by American Oliver Evans for the Philadelphia Board of Health, is "driven" 1½ miles from workshop to river on a wheeled under-carriage powered by a 5 hp steam engine.

1885 Gottlieb Daimler builds a motor cycle and Karl Benz, independently, constructs his first petrol engined three wheeler and lays the foundation for the modern motor industry.

1890 Panhard and Levassor start manufactore of cars in Paris under Daimler licence.

1894 The first motor competition, Paris–Rouen. A De Dion wins at an average 18.7 km/h.

1895 Lanchester brothers build first entirely British car.

1896 Locomotives on Highways Act raises speed limit in Britain from 4 to 14 mph (invariably restricted to 12 mph), prompting Harry Lawson to organize first London–Brighton Run to celebrate.

1897 The Automobile Club (later the R.A.C.) is formed.

1898 Chasseloup-Laubat in an electric car achieves 63.13 km/h, and the first Benz is imported into Britain.

1900 The Automobile Club organises a "1000 Miles Trial" round Britain. First National Automobile Show held in Madison Square Gardens, New York.

1903 Henry Ford and David Buick organise their own motor companies. Henry Ford Co. (Ford's second commercial enterprise) taken over by Henry Leland to become Cadillac. Motor Cars Act forces registration of British cars but raises speed limit to 20 mph.

1904 The first Rolls-Royce leaves the Manchester works.

1905 The Automobile Association is formed to combat police "speed traps".

1906 The first Rolls-Royce Silver Ghost is built, and a steam car achieves 205.24 km/h (127.56 mph) in America.

1907 Brooklands Motor Course opens at Weybridge, Surrey.

1908 Henry Ford produces his Model T.

1911 Chevrolet Motor Company started by William Durant.

1912 Cadillac standardize the Kettering self-starter.

1913 William Morris builds the first Morris Cowley.

1919 Rolls-Royce open their factory in Springfield, Massachusetts.

1922 Herbert Austin's "baby" Austin Seven is born.

1924 Walter Chrysler produces the first car to bear his name, and Cecil Kimber announces his Morris Garages Super Sports – the first M.G. Italy builds the first modern *autostrada* (motorway) between Milan and Varese.

1926 Germany's two oldest motor companies – Daimler and Benz – amalgamate to form Mercedes-Benz.

1927 The Lincoln Memorial Highway – from east to west coast of the United States – is completed. The last Ford Model T is built.

1929 Henry Segrave raises the world land-speed record to 372.38 km/h (231.44 mph) and is knighted for his achievement.

1930 The Veteran Car Club of Great Britain is formed. The Road Traffic Act introduces Third Party insurance for motor vehicles and abolishes 20 mph speed limit.

1934 Citroën introduce the advanced *"traction avant"* 7CV model; Chrysler and De Soto offer controversial "airflow" streamlining. In Germany the first *Autobahn* is built.

1935 The Antique Automobile Club of America – later to be the world's largest club for early vehicle enthusiasts – is formed.

1938 Rudolf Caracciola, driving a Mercedes-Benz, covers the flying kilometre at 432.7 km/h (268.9 mph) on the Frankfurt *Autobahn* – the highest speed then achieved on a public highway. Englishman Dick Seaman wins the German Grand Prix at Nürburgring in a Mercedes.

1941 The first Willys Jeeps delivered.

1942 America suspends all private car production.

1948 Arrival of the first Morris Minor designed by Alec Issigonis.

1949 After ten years of development the Boulanger-designed 2 CV Citroën appears.

1955 Citroën are again twenty years ahead with the introduction of their revolutionary DS19 model. Stirling Moss wins the Mille Miglia in a Mercedes.

1959 The first 69 mile section of the M1 London–Birmingham motorway opened by Transport Minister Ernest Marples. The Mini is introduced.

1960 D.A.F. introduce their belt-driven "automatic" car. The M.o.T. test is introduced.

1962 Graham Hill wins the Formula 1 World Championship.

1963 Rover-B.R.M. gas turbine car takes unofficial seventh place at Le Mans.

1964 Studebaker transfer all production from America to their Canadian plant.

1965 Jim Clark, driving a Lotus Ford, is the first British driver to win at Indianapolis, at an average speed of 242.453 km/h (150.686 mph). Craig Breedlove's "Spirit of America Sonic 1" breaks the world land speed record at 966.36 km/h (600.60 mph) at Bonneville.

1967 An overall speed limit of 70 mph is imposed in Britain and the "breathalyser" is introduced. Seat belts now compulsory in all new cars.

1970 Gary Gabelich sets up a new world land speed record of 1014.28 km/h (630.38 mph) in the Natural Gas Industry's "Blue Flame".

1971 One British family in every two now runs a car.

1972 On 15th February this year Volkswagen Beetle production exceeded the Model T Ford run of 15,007,033.

1973 The Arab–Israel war sparks off a fuel shortage, speedily followed by giant increases in the price of petrol and oil. Some Continental countries introduce "no motoring" week-ends. Britain imposes temporary economy overall speed limit of 50 mph.

1974 More manufacturers now concentrate upon safety in the design of cars following the earlier lead given by Ralph Nader in his book "Unsafe at any speed" which is sharply critical of American cars.

1975 British car registrations of 1.2 million during the year show a steady fall since 1973.

1976 Inflation is reflected in the price of a basic Mini at £1,587. compared with £497 on introduction in 1959. Top British seller is now the Ford Cortina.

INDEX

ACKNOWLEDGMENTS

The publishers would like to thank the following individuals and organisations for their kind permission to reproduce the photographs in this book. All photographs, unless otherwise credited, are from the Peter Roberts Collection.

After the Battle Magazine 62; Antique Automobile Association of the U.S.A. 30, 90; Aston Martin 98 above; Audi 86 below; *Autocar* 105 above, 116; British Leyland 35 below, 39 above, 47 above, 48 above, 63 above, 66–7, 70 below left, 71, 80, 86 below; Daimler-Benz 84–5, (Peter Roberts Collection) 122; Ford Archives, Henry Ford Museum, Dearborn, Michigan/Peter Roberts Collection 28 above left, 29 above; Ford Motor Co. 82–3, 89; General Motors 87 above, 101 below right; Kodak Museum 54–5 above; London Art Technical College 64–5, 76 above; Michelin (Peter Roberts Collection) 20 below; National Motor Museum 9 centre, 14–5, 17, 19 above right, 26–7 above, 32–3, 38 below left, 39 below, 42–3 below, 43, 45 above, 46–7 above and below, 49 above and below, 53 above, 56 above, 60–1, 99 above and below, 115 above and below, 118–9, 120; Tony Page 1, 119 centre; Peugeot Automobiles UK Ltd/Ted Bates Ltd 88 above; Charles Pocklington 46 above left; Porsche 85 inset; R.A.C. (Peter Roberts Collection) 18–19, 19 below right; Renault 84 below left inset, 88 below left; John Rigby 2–3, 78–9, 78 below right inset, 78 above inset, 78 below left inset, 84 below centre inset, 94–5, 95 inset, 100–1, 100–1, 114 below, (courtesy of Nick Butler) 74, 74–5; The Director, The Science Museum 8–9 below, 9 above, 24–5, 25 above right, 38 below right, 92; Shell U.K. Oil 45 below; Société Citroën 67 above; Tony Stone Associates 12–3 above, 20–1, 40–1, 56–7, 96–7; Colin Taylor 80–1, 81; Volkswagen (G.B.) 70 below right, 76–7, 87 below, 88 below right; N. Wright 31 above and below, 37 above, 56 below left, 59 below, 67 below, 76 below, 100 above.
Front jacket: Peter Roberts
Back jacket: Tony Page
Endpapers: Spectrum